History
ages 5-7

Pat Hoodless

Published by Scholastic Ltd,
Villiers House,
Clarendon Avenue,
Leamington Spa,
Warwickshire
CV32 5PR
www.scholastic.co.uk

Printed by Ebenezer Baylis & Son Ltd, Worcester
Text © 2001 Pat Hoodless
© 2001 Scholastic Ltd
1 2 3 4 5 6 7 8 9 0   1 2 3 4 5 6 7 8 9 0

Author

Pat Hoodless

Editor

Sarah Snashall

Assistant Editor

Dulcie Booth

Series designer

Lynne Joesbury

Designer

Erik Ivens

Illustrations

Beverly Curl

Cover illustration

Jon Berkley

British Library Cataloguing-in-Publication Data
A catalogue record for this book is available from the British Library.

ISBN 0-439-01818-8

Designed using Adobe Pagemaker

Contents

Acknowledgements

Little, Brown and Company London for drawings adapted from the Julius Work Calendar by Cotton Julius A VI circa AD 1020. Original manuscript in the British Library.

Little, Brown and Company (Inc.) for the use of 'A Party' by Laura E Richards from *Tirra Lirra* by Laura E Richards © 1932, by Laura E Richards, renewed 1960 by Hamilton Richards (1932, Little, Brown and Company (Inc) New York).

Peters Fraser & Dunlop Group for the use of 'First day at school' by Roger McGough from *You tell me* edited by Roger McGough © 1979, Roger McGough (1979, Kestrel Books).

Peters Fraser & Dunlop Group for the use of 'Going through the old photos' by Michael Rosen from *You tell me* edited by Roger McGough © 1979, Michael Rosen (1979, Kestrel Books).

The Random House Group for the use of 'A Growing Tale' from *To Read and to Tell* by Norah Montgomerie © 1974, Norah Montgomerie (1974, The Bodley Head).

The Society of Authors as the Literary Trustees of the Estate of Walter de la Mare for the use of 'Then' from *Peacock Pie* by Walter de la Mare © 1946, Walter de la Mare (1946, Unwin).

Every effort has been made to trace copyright holders and the publishers apologise for any omissions.

Introduction

Aims and purpose of the book

The texts included in this book have been selected for their potential in meeting the objectives of the National Curriculum for History at Key Stage 1 while also providing a wide range of opportunities for work related to the National Literacy Strategy. The numerous texts written in the past are in themselves a complete and inexhaustible resource for both teaching history and for work in literacy. These texts constitute the most meaningful, realistic link between the two subjects of history and English.

The book aims to provide teachers with suitable resources for combining teaching in history and literacy. This will allow for an economical use of time in a very busy primary curriculum. It will also create a meaningful context for work in literacy, where texts can be selected and used as part of the Literacy Hour and then explored in different ways in a history lesson. Some of the more challenging texts are beyond the individual reading level of many children, as is often the case with many history texts, but they can be made accessible in shared reading time and thus more readable in the history lesson itself. Shared reading enables the teacher to introduce texts of a wide variety, in forms quite different from the usual reading diet of the child at Key Stage 1. The benefits of using historical text in shared reading time are enormous; the child's experience of text is broadened, and their self-esteem is built up, along with their confidence to tackle new and unusual pieces of text.

Reading is an intrinsic part of learning history whether it is books about people and events or written evidence which people in the past left behind. The History National Curriculum describes these as 'sources of information' and some are the same as the 'genres' of the National Literacy Strategy. Obviously, the genres in literature are all to be found in historical texts. Teachers can therefore make links between the requirements of the History National Curriculum at Key Stage 1 and the National Literacy Strategy by choosing texts that help young children understand that there is a 'past' as well as a 'present'. Carefully selected texts and choice of appropriate history objectives can be used to promote the knowledge, skills and understanding required at Key Stage 1 and to address the relevant attainment targets, listed at the end of 'Curriculum 2000'.

Choice and breadth of texts

The texts included here have been selected from materials written at different times in the past and include fiction and poetry. Reading non-fiction texts is also obviously crucial to success in both literacy and history. These include letter and diary extracts, newspaper reports and extracts from history texts. Some are presented in their original form. Other more difficult texts have been simplified and presented as a transcription in modern English, while others have been specially written. As many small 'bites' of original historical source material as possible have been selected to strengthen the real links with the history curriculum.

Chapters have been organised under the general areas of study specified by the National Curriculum for History and also include texts related to the 'Scheme of Work' for history, published by the QCA, such as 'toys in the past'. The broad areas of study have been broken down, in some cases to allow more detailed attention, particularly in relation to different historical periods. Some chapters include items on periods in the past not covered by the National Curriculum at Key Stage 2, such as Edwardian and Stuart times and the Middle Ages, therefore providing an opportunity for children to work on additional periods in the more distant past.

Chapter One focuses on changes in children's own lives and the way of life of their family or others around them. These texts relate to the personal lives of children and other adults. The experiences are within their living memories and those of their families, taking them back to the 1950s and 60s. Chapter Two includes texts on the way of life of people in the more distant past who lived in the local area or elsewhere in Britain during Victorian times and the first half of the twentieth century. Chapter Three introduces texts about the way of life of people in a number of different periods in the very distant past, and includes items from or about Tudor, Stuart, Medieval, Saxon, Viking, Roman and Celtic times. Chapters Four and Five include texts related to the lives of significant men, women and children, and to significant events, drawn from the history of Britain and the wider world. These are wide ranging and an attempt has been made to include texts which involve people and events from different cultures and areas of the world.

The texts have also been related to the 'knowledge, skills and understanding' required by the National Curriculum. Chronology plays an important part in many of the suggested activities related to the texts, both in terms of placing events and spans of time on timelines, and also in terms of providing opportunities for children to learn and practise skills in sequencing. Key concepts, such as similarity and difference, continuity and change, and causation have been highlighted. The notion of interpretation is often apparent in the texts themselves, which contain examples of how different points of view can influence attitudes, actions and historical sources. The skills involved in using sources are particularly significant when working with texts. The identification of key points in a text and the ability to make inferences are two important skills, which are discussed in the teachers' notes and also highlighted in the suggested activities and discussion points. Finally, a wide variety of ways in which history can be communicated is addressed in the suggested history and cross-curricular activities, ranging from role-play and drama to modelling and book-making.

The progression implicit in the history curriculum, in terms of moving from the familiar and personal, towards the more distant past, is reflected in the book. An assumption has been made that children in Year One will mainly study their own experiences, family, locality and familiar events, such as anniversaries. Texts in the early chapters reflect this and are, on the whole, at an easier reading level. By the end of Key Stage 1, it is assumed that children will be studying more distant times in the past. The texts in these chapters are therefore often at a higher readability level and some are very challenging. A variety of reading levels is still provided within each chapter however, to allow for the wide range of reading levels among children within each year group.

Teaching with texts as part of a history unit of work

The book consists of a selection of texts for use in teaching Key Stage 1 history, and the chapters have been organised on this basis in a largely chronological sequence. The texts could be used for whole class, group or individual work in history building on the comprehension work done as shared reading with the whole class within the Literacy Hour. Background information on the texts, the texts themselves and teachers' notes are provided for each area of study outlined in the history curriculum for Key Stage 1. This background information on the sources is intended to provide teachers with further detail for use in setting the context, providing further information for the children during discussion, and for planning extension activities related to the text. The teachers' notes are not intended to be seen as lesson plans, but are written for flexible use in the classroom. They aim to provide ideas for developing activities in both history and guided reading, group and individual work, which could be used in the middle section of the Literacy Hour. A range of objectives is suggested for each text, from which the teacher can select as appropriate to achieve a specific focus for individual lessons or activities.

Many of the texts are either original or adapted from original documents. They will put children into immediate, firsthand contact with the experiences, emotions and thoughts of those who wrote, or were involved in them. Children will have the opportunity to read words written by famous figures from the past, such as Mary Seacole, writing about her own childhood games and fantasies, or by inventors like John Logie Baird, expressing his excitement at seeing the very first ever television pictures. Similarly, the words exchanged between the first men arriving on the Moon and those back on earth enable children to appreciate the tension and emotion felt on that momentous occasion.

The texts, however, are intended to be used as part of a wider historical theme or topic. The children need to go beyond what is written in the text, to appreciate the wider context in which it was written. They are seen more as a starting point or stimulus for further discussion and investigation, in which links can be made with other periods, events and people. Some texts can be used alongside other sources of evidence, such as artefacts, pictures, photographs, historic sites or oral testimony. Others could be used to stimulate questions and curiosity.

Teaching with texts and the National Literacy Strategy

As has been mentioned above, many texts from the past are difficult to read. However, the chance to use such texts as part of the Literacy Hour will alleviate many of these problems. Working with a skilful teacher, the meaning of such texts and archaic words can be drawn out and discussed with the children. Support can be offered at the stage of reading through the text as part of the whole class activity. There is also time to clarify meanings during the discussion of each text, when questions requiring comprehension work can be used to good effect.

Historical sources encompass every genre described in the National Literacy Strategy, and as such, provide perhaps the greatest resource for the selection of texts.

Examples of text genres common to both history and literacy have been selected to cover relevant literacy objectives, and to provide a stimulus for further literacy activities. These include:

   stories with familiar settings, and stories and rhymes with predictable patterns
   signs, labels and captions, for example, those that might be encountered at a historic site or museum and place names
   lists such as the vocabulary associated with instructions or personal property
   playground chants and rhymes from the past
   script such as the dialogue between groups of people
   information texts which recount observation of visits or events, such as newspaper reports
   letters and messages
◆ instructions such as simple recipes from the past
   poems with familiar settings or by significant children's authors

◆ autobiographical details or personal recollections of 'significant people'

◆ hymns

◆ chronological writing in diary form

◆ reference text, such as an encyclopedia entry.

Many are the same, or are closely related to the major genres identified in the National Literacy Strategy: information, narrative, instruction, persuasive and reference text. These categories, however, are not always definitive and there is some overlap between them. Consequently, some of the historical sources have a less well-defined relationship with any one particular genre, and may relate to more than one. The closest and clearest links have been identified in the reference grid on pages 9–10.

The texts create openings in different ways for detailed word- and sentence-level work, but particularly lend themselves as models for further text-level work in the form of shared writing.

Using the book in planning

The texts in this book, as has been mentioned above, are not intended to serve as schemes of work or lesson plans. They are intended only as suggestions for teaching strategies and as the beginnings of a resource bank of texts for work in literacy which relates to the history curriculum. The book is designed therefore to be flexible and could be used in a number of different ways, such as:

◆ 'Discussing the text' as part of a shared reading session, to draw out the meaning and ensure the full understanding of the text by the children.

◆ Using the text in a different way as a starting point for work in history, but this time as a source of historical information. Once the initial problems of comprehension and reading difficulty are overcome, then it will be possible to move beyond the text itself and begin to appreciate its historical context and significance.

◆ Many of the texts create opportunities for further research.

◆ Incorporating examples from the 'History activities' into a unit of work or a lesson plan.

◆ Using some of the written tasks related to the history lesson as part of the literacy hour group activities.

◆ Developing cross-curricular work in the process of children communicating the results of their enquires.

By working on related material in both areas of the curriculum, children's motivation, understanding and subject-related skills will be considerably enhanced.

EXTRACT	GENRE	HISTORY LEARNING OBJECTIVES	LITERACY LEARNING OBJECTIVES	PAGE
Changes in children's own lives				
Mrs Hunter's house	Narrative text; modern non-fiction	H 1a, 1b, 2b, 4a Breadth of study 6a	◆ To begin to recognise ordered sequence. ◆ To collect time-related words.	12
Butlin's holiday camp	Information text	H 1a, 1b, 2a, 2b, 4a Breadth of study 6a	◆ To recognise words within words. ◆ To identify speech marks.	15
An old-fashioned alphabet	Reference text; non-fiction from the past	H 1b, 2b, 4a Breadth of study 6a	◆ To secure alphabetic knowledge and alphabetic order. ◆ To read and spell words with initial consonant clusters.	18
A peg doll	Instruction text	H 1a, 1b, 2a Breadth of study 6a	◆ To use standard forms of verbs. ◆ To write simple instructions.	21
The clothes people wore	Information text; labels	H 1a, 1b, 2b, 4a Breadth of study 6a	◆ To read and use captions. ◆ To use time-related vocabulary.	25
First day at school	(1) Modern fiction (2) Poem	H 1a, 1b, 2a, 3, 4a Breadth of study 6a	◆ To recognise capital letters. ◆ To write stories or poems using their knowledge of settings.	28
Going through the old photos	Rhyming poem	H 1a, 1b, 2b, 3, 4a Breadth of study 6a	◆ To practise and secure the ability to rhyme. ◆ To identify simple questions and use question marks.	32
A party	Rhyming poem	H 1b, 2b, 3, 4a Breadth of study 6a	◆ To practise and secure the ability to rhyme. ◆ To recognise the uses of capital letters.	35
A growing tale	Narrative text; modern fiction	H 1a, 1b, 2a Breadth of study 6a	◆ To begin to recognise and write an ordered sequence of events. ◆ To use time-related vocabulary.	38
A royal family tree	Reference text; a chart	H 1a, 1b, 3 Breadth of study 6a	◆ To write using capital letters. ◆ To read and understand a chart.	41
Life in the more distant past				
Then	Rhyming poem	H 1a, 1b, 4a Breadth of study 6b	◆ To recognise common spelling patterns. ◆ To identify and discuss patterns of rhythm and rhyme. ◆ To use awareness of grammar to decipher new or unfamiliar words.	45
Working class meals, 1833	Information text; a report from the past	H 1b, 2b, 4a Breadth of study 6b	◆ To make simple lists. ◆ To understand the uses of note-making. ◆ To write non-chronological reports.	48
The land of counterpane	Poem from the past	H 2b, 3, 4a Breadth of study 6b	◆ To collect new words linked to a particular topic. ◆ To write descriptive sentences.	51
An old Victorian bottle	Report text; labels	H 1a, 1b, 4a Breadth of study 6b	◆ To identify questions. ◆ To write labels and non-fiction texts.	54
A good play	Rhyming poem	H 3, 4a, 4b Breadth of study 6b	◆ To identify and discuss patterns of rhythm and rhyme. ◆ To find examples of words that link sentences.	57
Washday at home	Narrative text; action rhyme from the past	H 1a, 1b, 2b, 4a, 5 Breadth of study 6b	◆ To identify and discuss patterns of rhythm and rhyme. ◆ To recognise common spelling patterns.	60
An old-fashioned lesson	Instruction text; non-fiction from the past	H 1a, 2b, 4a, 5 Breadth of study 6b	◆ To practise and secure alphabetic knowledge. ◆ To recognise the uses of capital letters.	63
A message from the King	Persuasive text; non-fiction	H 1a, 2b, 4a Breadth of study 6b	◆ To recognise the uses of capital letters. ◆ To collect words linked to a particular topic.	66
Life in the very distant past				
Exploring a Celtic house	Narrative text; explanation about a Celtic house	H 1b, 2b, 4a Breadth of study 6b	◆ To write captions. ◆ To understand the need for grammatical agreement. ◆ To collect words linked to a particular topic.	70
Roman soldiers	Information text; descriptions of two Roman soldiers	H 1b, 4a, 5 Breadth of study 6b	◆ To write simple captions and lists. ◆ To collect words linked to a particular topic. ◆ To use awareness of grammar to decipher new or unfamiliar words.	73
Julius work calendar	Information text/captions; an instruction manual for monks	H 1a, 1b, 3, 4a Breadth of study 6b	◆ To recognise the uses of capital letters. ◆ To begin to recognise ordered sequence. ◆ To discriminate syllables in reading.	76
Viking place names	Information/reference text places names from the past	H 1b, 4a, 5 Breadth of study 6b	◆ To recognise common spelling patterns. ◆ To recognise the uses of capital letters. ◆ To discriminate syllables in reading.	80
The first castles	Information text; labelled illustrations	H 1a, 2b, 3, 4a Breadth of study 6b	◆ To write simple captions. ◆ To recognise the uses of capital letters. ◆ To write sustained stories using their knowledge of settings.	83

EXTRACT	GENRE	SUBJECT LEARNING OBJECTIVES	LITERACY LEARNING OBJECTIVES	PAGE
Jumbles	Instruction text; a modern version of a medieval recipe	H 1b, 2b, 4a Breadth of study 6b	◆ To write simple lists and instructions. ◆ To collect words linked to a particular topic. ◆ To write non-chronological texts.	86
A Tudor letter	Recount text: a Tudor letter (modern and original versions)	H 1b, 2b, 4a, 4b, 5 Breadth of study 6b	◆ To collect words linked to a particular topic. ◆ To make simple notes from non-fiction text. ◆ To write sustained stories using their knowledge of settings.	89
A poor man's property	Information text; inventory from the past	H 1a, 1b, 2b, 4a Breadth of study 6b	◆ To collect words linked to a particular topic. ◆ To understand the use of note form in lists. ◆ To write non-chronological texts.	93
Ring-a-ring o' roses	Rhyming poem; an action rhyme from the past	H 1a, 2b, 4a Breadth of study 6b	◆ To practise and secure the ability to rhyme. ◆ To organise non-chronological text in chart form. ◆ To write sustained stories using their knowledge of settings.	96
A harvest hymn	Rhyming poem; a hymn from the past	H 2b, 3, 4a Breadth of study 6b	◆ To identify and discuss patterns of rhythm and rhyme. ◆ To recognise common spelling patterns. ◆ To recognise the uses of capital letters and full stops.	99

The lives of significant men and women

EXTRACT	GENRE	SUBJECT LEARNING OBJECTIVES	LITERACY LEARNING OBJECTIVES	PAGE
Life in Wales, by Gerald of Wales	Recount text: modern translation of middle ages text	H 1b, 2b, 4a, 5 Breadth of study 6c	◆ To collect words linked to a particular topic. ◆ To write non-chronological texts.	103
Mary Queen of Scots	Reference text; a timechart	H 1a, 1b, 2b, 4a, 5 Breadth of study 6c	◆ To recognise the uses of capital letters and full stops in writing sentences. ◆ To write chronological accounts. ◆ To understand the need for grammatical agreement.	106
George Frideric Handel	Recount text; modern fictitious letter	H 1a, 1b, 2b, 4a, 5 Breadth of study 6c	◆ To recognise the uses of capital letters. ◆ To use awareness of grammar to decipher new or unfamiliar words. ◆ To write non-chronological texts.	109
Nelson's first farewell	Recount text; fiction recount from 19th-century magazine	H 1a, 1b, 2b, 3, 4a Breadth of study 6c	◆ To identify speech marks. ◆ To write non-chronological texts.	112
George Stephenson's *Rocket*	Narrative text; recount of historical event	1a, 1b, 2b, 4a, 5 Breadth of study 6c	◆ To collect words linked to a particular topic. ◆ To recognise the uses of capital letters. ◆ To organise chronological text in chart form.	115
Grace Darling	Narrative text; recount of historical event	H 1b, 4a, 5 Breadth of study 6c	◆ To recognise significant words linked to a topic. ◆ To understand sequential relationships in stories. ◆ To begin to recognise and write an ordered sequence.	118
Mary Seacole	Narrative text; autobiography from the past	H 1a, 1b, 2b, 4a, 5 Breadth of study 6c	◆ To understand the distinction between fact and fiction. ◆ To understand the need for grammatical agreement.	122
Mahatma Gandhi	Information text; a newspaper report	H 1a, 1b, 4a, 5 Breadth of study 6c	◆ To understand the distinction between fact and fiction. ◆ To write non-fiction texts; use of layout and fonts.	125

Past events

EXTRACT	GENRE	SUBJECT LEARNING OBJECTIVES	LITERACY LEARNING OBJECTIVES	PAGE
A famous journey	Narrative text; modern translation of 15th-century text	H 1a, 1b, 3, 4a, 5 Breadth of study 6d	◆ To recognise the uses of capital letters. ◆ To understand the use of note form. ◆ To write non-fiction text using text read as a model.	129
Gunpowder treason and plot	Persuasive text; traditional rhyme	H 1b, 3, 4a, 5 Breadth of study 6d	◆ To identify and discuss patterns of rhythm and rhyme. ◆ To collect words linked to a particular topic. ◆ To write simple playscripts.	133
'In Flanders Fields' : a poem for Remembrance Day	Persuasive text; a poem from the past	H 1a, 1b, 3, 4a, 5 Breadth of study 6d	◆ To use awareness of grammar to decipher new or unfamiliar words. ◆ To identify and discuss patterns of rhythm and rhyme. ◆ To write poetry of a similar type.	136
The first television pictures	Reference text; an encyclopedia entry	H 1a, 1b, 2b, 4a, 5 Breadth of study 6d	◆ To identify the main events in the text. ◆ To collect words linked to a particular topic and make a class dictionary. ◆ To understand the use of alphabetical order and abbreviation in reference text. ◆ To understand the use of speech marks.	139
Moon landing	Narrative/ instruction text; a conversation between astronauts and ground control	H 1a, 1b, 3, 4a, 5 Breadth of study 6d	◆ To identify the main events in the text. ◆ To understand the use of speech marks. ◆ To use awareness of grammar to decipher new or unfamiliar words. ◆ To write non-fiction text using text read as a model.	142

Changes in children's own lives

The notion of making history understandable and relevant to young children by starting with their own life and experiences has been a part of the National Curriculum for history since its inception. Implicit in this is the assumption that the study of history moves back in time, gradually extending and refining the young child's awareness, first of all that there is a past within their own experience, and then that there are different times in the past. At this point, teaching begins to move beyond the living memory of the children and the adults around them. This approach is based on a substantial body of research evidence that suggests that even young children can begin to understand complex concepts if they are couched in appropriate contexts within their own remembered experience. One example of this is the teaching of the concept of time. Whereas a child of five or six is unlikely to be able to chronologically sequence dates and events from national history, they will be able to correctly order events from their own daily routine. This chapter, therefore, includes texts that are closely related to the everyday experiences of young children, such as birthday parties, looking at family photos or going on holiday.

Change, chronology and sequence are key concepts that play a large part in many of these texts. Children will be able to remember how many candles they had on their last birthday cake, like Tim in 'A growing tale', and will realise that Tim is younger than they are. 'Mrs Hunter's house' also involves sequencing and chronology, but over a much longer period of time. They may be able to remember their first day at school and be able to compare it with the two versions here. Also, the notion of measuring time through passing generations in families can be introduced through 'Going through the old photos' or 'A royal family tree'.

Some of the texts provide an opportunity to think about change and continuity. These texts include 'A party', where the food children eat has probably changed, 'A peg doll', which is very different from a modern doll, and 'The clothes people wore', which shows fashions from the 1960s. Familiar objects or activities can be readily used for the children to compare 'then' and 'now'.

Sequence is, of course, a major feature of work in literacy, and this can be developed through the use of both poetry and prose texts in this chapter. Rhyme, subject-related vocabulary, aspects of grammar and punctuation and spelling patterns can also be touched upon in Literacy Hour activities.

Mrs Hunter's house

Genre
*recount text;
modern
non-fiction*

A hundred years ago there was a track that led to a quarry. Our neighbour, old Mrs Bell, can remember what it was like when the stone cottages were built along the track.

Years later, a row of new brick houses was built. My family moved into the street when I was six. Our house had a long garden at the back.

My father grew vegetables in it. My mother had a gas cooker. I thought it was very clean and modern. All the new houses had bathrooms. We had electric lights, but we still had coal fires to keep the house warm. There were lots of new

electrical things to buy. My mother liked looking at all the advertisements, but she did not have enough money to buy new things.

Now, in my own house, we have many modern electrical things, like a television, a computer and a telephone. My grown-up children have mobile phones of their own.

Mrs Hunter's house

Area of study
Changes in children's own lives and the way of life of their family or others around them.

History learning objectives

- To place events, people and objects in chronological order (1a).
- To use common words and phrases related to the passing of time (1b).
- To identify differences between ways of life at different times (2b).
◆ To find out about the past from text (4a).

Background notes

This extract looks at some of the aspects of houses and homes over three generations. Mrs Hunter's mother is of present-day children's great-grandparents' generation. Mrs Hunter, the narrator, is their grandparents' generation, since she has 'grown-up' children. Mrs Hunter's children are probably the generation of the parents of the children in the class.

Mrs Hunter talks about her home when she was a child and also about her present home. The extract is useful for instigating talk about the different age groups in society and for looking at generations within families. It also opens up opportunities for further work on similarities and differences between homes in the past and the present day, building up children's awareness of change and continuity, key concepts in history.

The text makes use of words relating to the passing of time, particularly those that indicate a sequence of events. This aspect of work at Key Stage 1 is common to both literacy and history. While this extract is an example of oral history, it is useful in the Literacy Hour for teaching about first-person accounts. Young children will be able to relate readily to it and will be able to produce accounts of their own.

Vocabulary

Hundred; cottages; electric; years; brick; lights; ago; houses; coal; when; gas; now; cooker.

Discussing the text

- Read through the text to and with the children and look at the illustrations.
- Ask the children what this text is telling them about.
◆ Can the children say who is talking in this extract? Explain to the children that it is written in the first person.
- Ask the class to count how many times the word *I* is used.
- Ask the children to point out other words that tell us that it is written in the first person. (For example, *my, we*.)
- Ask the children to suggest why Mrs Hunter is telling this account. (She is explaining to the children how houses have changed.)
◆ Ask: *How old was Mrs Hunter when she and her family moved into their new house?*
- Ask: *What sort of things does Mrs Hunter have in her house now?*
- Ask the children which of Mrs Hunter's homes is most like their home. What are the children's homes like? Do they have coal fires? Do they have electric lights? Do they have gas cookers?
- Ask: *What did Mrs Hunter have in her house when she was a child? Did she have a computer or a television? How was her house kept warm?* How are the children's houses kept warm today?

History activities

◆ Discuss with the children how some things at home change and other things stay the same, and begin to identify these similarities and differences.

◆ Make a simple chart showing things that have stayed the same, such as cookers and things that are new and different, such as computers. Complete the chart as part of a shared writing activity.

◆ There is an even older house in the story. Which is it? How long ago was it built? On a very simple sequence line, ask volunteers to place each house mentioned in the story in the correct place.

◆ If possible, visit sites or museums which have reconstructions of houses from the past, such as the Black Country Museum in Dudley, West Midlands, or Larkhill Place, Salford Museum, Manchester. In many of these reconstructions it is possible to see both the outside of the houses and the interiors of some of the rooms.

◆ For homework, ask the children to draw some pictures of their own homes and bring them to school.

◆ Collect books and other resources on houses and homes in the past for reference and for the children to use to draw pictures to compare with present-day homes.

◆ Discuss the passing of time with the children. Can they remember moving? Can they remember getting a new computer? Ask the children to talk to their parents about when they were children.

Further literacy ideas

◆ Ask the children to pick out the words which tell us the order in which the different houses were built, for example *a hundred years ago*, *when I was six*, *now*. Give the class other words that describe chronological sequence, such as *first*, *next*, *then*. Ask the children to think of a series of events using these words in order.

◆ Point out the use of capital letters and full stops in the text to reinforce knowledge and understanding of sentence structure.

◆ Notice additional uses of capital letters, such as in titles like *Mrs*. Discuss other titles, such as *Mr* and *Miss*, modelling the use of the capital letter through writing it on the board for the children to read.

◆ Discuss with the class the difference between fiction and non-fiction, and encourage them to consider which this extract is.

◆ Working either during shared writing or guided writing time, demonstrate to the children how to write in the first person, and encourage them to write a brief personal account of their own in the same style.

Butlin's holiday camp

Genre
information
text

The normal day at Butlin's begins at 7.45 when the camp radio gives a hearty rise-and-shine call to the camp. The voice is cheerful, but relentless, as it recites:

> "Good morning, campers. It is a lovely day and the sun is shining [or, the weather has let us down] so show a leg you lads and lasses, rub the sleep out of your eyes and prepare for another grand day of fun, another Butlin's jolliday."

A visitor said campers were "expected to take part each morning in army-style keep-fit exercises. They do so. And they like it." Billy Butlin said the secret of his success was that he gave the campers what they wanted. "They come back year after year. That is my test."

(Source)/Science & Society Picture Library

Butlin's holiday camp

Area of study
Changes in children's own lives and the way of life of their family or others around them.

History learning objectives

◆ To place events, people and objects in chronological order (1a).

◆ To use common words and phrases related to the passing of time (1b).

◆ To recognise why people did things and why events happened… (2a).

◆ To identify differences between ways of life at different times (2b).

◆ To find out about the past from text about changes in their own lives (4a).

Background notes

Holiday camps such as *Butlin's* became popular after the war. Ordinary working people began to get holiday pay and could afford a break at the seaside. Many of them went to holiday camps like these. The camps remained popular for many years and some are still busy today. Some of the children's own grandparents, parents, and some children themselves might have been to a holiday camp. The topic, therefore, will be one that most children can talk about at home, and relate to closely through their families' experiences, if not their own.

Nowadays, many children are used to travelling further afield, and many go abroad, often on package tours by air. Holidays have changed in many ways, and this extract gives a chance to compare modern holidays with this example of a holiday camp regime just after the Second World War. It provides an insight into how reports were written in the 1940s, in a somewhat 'jolly' style. For Literacy Hour work, it provides a good example of direct speech and the use of speech marks.

Vocabulary

Holiday; camp; campers; radio; fun; keep-fit.

Discussing the text

◆ Read through the text to and with the children.

◆ What kind of writing do the children think this is?

◆ Who do the children think wrote it and why?

◆ Why is some of the writing divided off from the rest?

◆ Encourage the children to notice the direct speech marks. Discuss why they are there.

◆ Can the children say what time the campers had to get up? Ask the children: *Why did they have to get up at this time?*

◆ Ask: *What kind of day did the camp radio say they would all have? Did this depend on the weather?* Point out the word *jolliday* to the children. Have they heard it before? Do they think it is a real word? Can they work out how it has been made up?

◆ Do the children think their parents would enjoy *army-style keep-fit exercises* early every morning on holiday? Why not? What do the children think they would prefer to do?

◆ Look at the photograph and draw the children's attention to the chalets. Have any of them ever stayed in a holiday chalet?

◆ Have the children been on holiday recently? Did they stay in a holiday camp or did they go somewhere different?

◆ List on the flip chart or board all the places children visit on their holidays now.

History activities

◆ Collect books, pictures and other resources about the 1940s and 50s. Holiday camp advertisements and brochures would also be very useful for reference, as well as present-day information about holidays. Get the children to use these resources to cut out or draw pictures of past holidays and present ones.

Make a wall display or chart for each period, including a good selection of pictures.

Use the display when working with groups of children. Encourage them to observe closely and identify things that have changed and things that have stayed the same. Talk about what they see in the pictures, giving the names of things they may not recognise or know about.

◆ During a PE lesson, re-enact the activities described in this extract, inventing keep-fit activities such as the campers might have used.

◆ Mark on the map all the places the children have visited, and include the map in the wall display about holidays past and present.

◆ Using a large map of the world, identify some of the places the children have travelled to. Discuss how they travel nowadays. Compare this information with the places people went to in the past and the transport they used. For example, in Britain in the 1940s and 50s people travelled by car, bus or train.

Further literacy ideas

Point out to the children how words can be made from other words, for example *camp* and *camper*. Give the children some other words, such as *read, build, sing, play,* or *speak,* to turn into new words by adding -er.

Ask the children to point to the words that were spoken by someone on the camp radio. How do we know these were the actual words that were said? Point out the speech marks. Look at other examples of speech marks in different texts and books.

Working with the whole class, make up some questions about holidays which could be answered by reference to the class collection of books on this period.

Discuss the differences between fact and fiction and ask the children which kind of writing appears in this report.

Make a simple writing frame in which to list things that have changed and things that have stayed the same. Working with the whole class, model ways of completing the chart, then encourage the children to add other ideas of their own.

An old-fashioned alphabet

Genre
reference text;
non-fiction
from the past

A – ark	**B** – boat	**C** – car	**D** – drum
E – easel	**F** – forest	**G** – gate	**H** – hive
I – inn	**J** – jug	**K** – kettle	**L** – lighthouse
M – marrow	**N** – newt	**O** – owl	**P** – pig
Q – quince	**R** – rhubarb	**S** – ship	**T** – train
U – umbrella	**V** – vane	**W** – wheel-barrow	**X** – xmas
Y – yacht	**Z** – zebra		

An old-fashioned alphabet

Area of study
Changes in children's own lives and the way of life of their family or others around them.

History learning objectives
◆ To use common words and phrases related to the passing of time (1b).
◆ To identify differences between ways of life at different times (2b).
◆ To find out about the past from pictures and text (4a).

Background notes
This alphabet book dates back to the time of the children's grandparents or great-grandparents. The choice of vocabulary is very old-fashioned, for example *ark*, *easel*, *marrow* and *quince*. Some of the items, for example *kettle*, *ship* and *train* are still in use today, but the illustrations show how they have changed since the 1940s.

This text gives an opportunity for the children to identify words and objects from the past, while at the same time, practising their alphabet and reinforcing their knowledge and use of initial letters and initial consonant clusters.

Vocabulary
Ark; boat; easel; forest; hive; inn; jug; kettle; lighthouse; marrow; newt; owl; pig; quince; rhubarb; ship; train; umbrella; vane; wheelbarrow; xmas; yacht; zebra.

Discussing the text
◆ After reading through the alphabet with the class, explain to the children what it is. Tell them that these are the sorts of words children would have used to remember their alphabet many years ago.
◆ Ask the children what the text looks like. Explain that it is like a list – a list of letters and words. There is one word for each letter of the alphabet.
◆ Ask the children if they know their alphabet and rehearse it with them.
◆ Discuss with the children the difference between letters and words. Ask individual children to point first to letters, then to words.
◆ Do the children have alphabet books at home? Explain how they are sometimes called *ABC* books.
◆ Discuss with the children any words they don't know. Can they work out what the words mean from the pictures?
◆ Notice the long words and the short words. Get them to pick out the short words and read them. Ask the children if they can read any of the long words too.
◆ Point out the illustrations for *kettle*, *ship* and *train*. Do these objects look like this today?
◆ Ask if any of the children can sing the alphabet and do this with the class.

History activities
◆ Collect a variety of alphabet books from different times in the past together with some modern ones. Ask the children, or their parents/carers if they would look out old alphabet books they may have at home and lend these to the class for a short time.
◆ Organise an 'alphabet-book table', grouping the new and old books.
◆ With the whole class, in groups, or as individuals, ask the children to compare an old book with a

new one. Choose fairly obvious examples, if possible, the first few times this activity is carried out. Encourage the children to look very carefully at the details. Once the children have decided which is old and which is new, ask them to tell you why they think this. What can they see that tells them this? Try to get as many different reasons as possible from the children, moving on to more subtle differences, such as the content of the pictures, the style of the illustrations, the old-fashioned objects and words that are used.

◆ Make some activity sheets for the children on which you have cut and pasted some old-fashioned pictures cut from unwanted alphabet books. Include a list of appropriate initial letters at the bottom of the sheet. Working with small groups, look at the pictures and ask the children to name the pictures and then give the initial sound for each word. From the list at the foot of the page, the children select the correct initial sounds for the pictures and either draw lines to join them or write the letters next to them. Discuss whether the pictures are old-fashioned or new.

◆ Using a set of alphabet cards, challenge the children to make up a phrase for each one, such as *a is for ant.*

◆ Using old-fashioned pictures cut from old magazines, make a class alphabet for the wall. The children can colour in large initial letters for the wall display. Alternatively, make an old-fashioned class *ABC* book.

Further literacy ideas

◆ Give each child a large card with a letter of the alphabet printed on it. Get them to form a 'human' alphabet and say their own letter in turn.

◆ Pick out from the vocabulary list the words with a single initial letter sound, such as *boat, kettle* Write these on the board and ask the children to say the initial letter sound, then read the word.

◆ Select words from the vocabulary list with initial consonant clusters, such as *drum, ship, train.* Write these on the board and ask for volunteers to say the initial clusters, then read the whole word. See if the children can give other words beginning with the same clusters.

◆ Using shared writing time, ask the children to give new words beginning with each letter of the alphabet. Provide the class with a copy of the alphabet in list form and model the writing of these words next to each letter.

◆ Display one picture from a modern alphabet book and one from an old-fashioned book. Encourage the children to write about the differences, for example what 'clues' make one picture look old and the other new.

A peg doll

Genre
instruction
text

You will need:

an old-fashioned wooden clothes peg
with a round head
a pipe cleaner
paper
scraps of material
needle and thread
wool
beads
fine wool or thread
scraps of thin lace or ribbon

What to do:

1. Take the wooden clothes
peg. The round 'head' of the
peg will be the doll's head and
the rest will be the body.

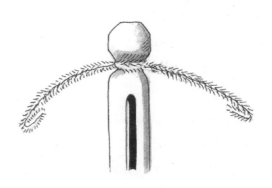

2. Wind the pipe cleaner around
the neck of the peg to create
arms.

3. On a piece of paper draw a
pattern for the doll's dress. It is
best if it is a long dress, going
from below the head to the
bottom of the peg. It will also
need long sleeves.

4. Fold the cloth double and pin
the pattern on the cloth – lining
up the pattern with the top of the
cloth. Cut out the dress.

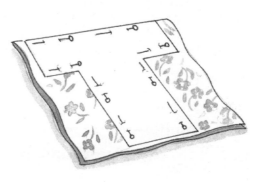

5. Sew the two sides together.

6. Cut a hole in the top of the dress to create a neck.

7. Pull the dress over the peg. Once the dress is in place, fasten it at the neck with a few stitches.

8. Make two small hands in thick cloth or felt. Glue or sew these to the end of each pipe-cleaner arm.

9. Use the wool to make the doll some hair. Stitch the hair together and glue it to the doll's head.

10. Make eyes and a mouth either from paper or felt. You could use small beads for the eyes. Glue these to the doll's head.

11. Using fine wool or thread, make eyebrows and eyelashes for your doll. Glue these on.

12. Add details to the dress, such as a lace collar, a belt or bow, or some pockets. You may like to finish off your peg doll with a smart hat.

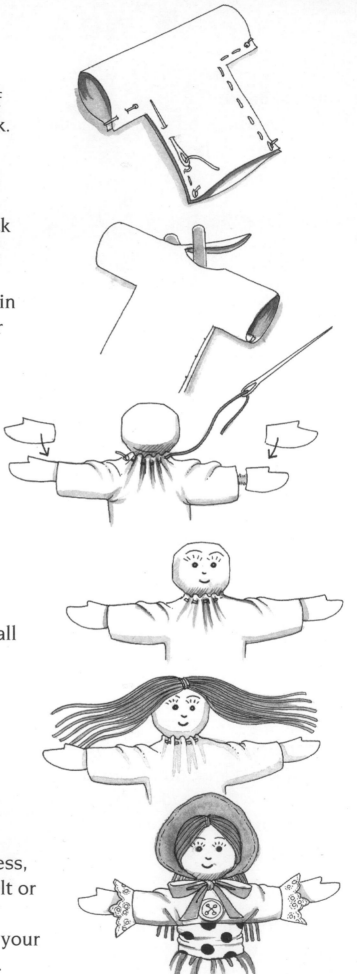

A peg doll

Area of study
Changes in children's own lives and the way of life of their family or others around them.

History learning objectives

- To place events… in chronological order (1a).
- To use common words and phrases related to the passing of time (1b).
- To recognise why people did things and why events happened… (2a).

Background notes

Peg dolls were popular in Victorian times, and became popular again in the 20th century – within the memory of children's family members. In the years following the Second World War, many things were still very scarce. Toys were often quite expensive and working-class mothers had to resort to whatever was at hand to make toys and games to keep their children occupied. Often, simple household items, such as pegs, would be used for making toys. These pegs were wooden and quite large to a small child. Sometimes, two pegs would be pushed together to form a cross, which would become an aeroplane. A mother with spare time would make more elaborate things with a spare peg, such as a doll.

This instruction-text genre provides an opportunity to look at categories of words such as verbs. The instructions are simple and, if an old-fashioned wooden peg can be found, the doll itself can easily be made to accompany children's work arising from the text. The peg doll can be compared with a modern doll, enabling the children to compare toys that their grandparents may remember with the kinds of toys they themselves have now.

Vocabulary

Take; fold; glue; cut; make; fasten; push; sew; measure.

Discussing the text

- Read the instructions to the class.
- Ask the children what this text is telling them to do.
- What do they notice about how it is set out on the page?
- Can they say why each instruction starts on a new line?
- Why do they think the instructions are numbered?
- Do they know what a clothes peg is? Have some examples ready to show them.
- Look back at details in the instructions. Re-read with the class particular instructions, pointing out the woollen ball for a head and the dress for the body.
- Would they like to have a toy like this or do they prefer their modern toys?

History activities

- Explain how, during and after the Second World War, in their grandparents' and great-grandparents' days, children had to play with toys made from everyday things such as clothes pegs. Tell them how they would use these as toys or make toys from them.
- ◆ Make a peg doll to accompany the text.
- ◆ Show the children a selection of dolls from different periods – a doll from the 1940s or 50s (their grandparents' childhood), a doll from the 1960s or 70s (their parents' childhood) and a present-day doll. Discuss the differences between the dolls. Which doll would the children most like to play with?

Mix them up and ask individual children to put them into the right 'time' order. Ask them to explain why they have put them in this order; how do they know?

◆ Collect other toys from different times in the past and organise activities for pairs, groups or individuals to try their hand at sequencing them chronologically. This can be a useful assessment task, in which you can easily observe their understanding of sequence and chronology. You can also assess their skill in using time-related vocabulary when asking them why they put the toys in a particular order.

◆ Make a class toy shop or toy museum. Label the toys in the display, with their names and with generation that they come from, for example grandparents, parents, or the children themselves. The children can then try to match the correct labels to the toys. Allow time for the children to play with the less valuable toys.

◆ The children can also work in pairs to sort the toys into different groups, according to their ages. They could make separate 'windows' for each group in their toy shop.

Further literacy ideas

◆ Pick out some examples of verbs from the text, such as *push*, *sew*, *cut*. Get the children to read them from the board and to perform the actions the verbs are telling them to do.

◆ Create sets of verb cards – pairs of illustration cards and word cards. Ask the children to work in pairs or individually to match the words to the pictures.

◆ Make a simple cloze-procedure sheet, providing the missing verbs at the bottom for the children to insert in the correct sentences. This activity could also be done on the computer, using a suitable word-processing programme.

◆ Give the children a set of instructions, set out in the same way as in the extract, but with no numbers and no capital letters. Ask the children to number the instructions and put in the missing capital letters at the beginning of each one. Provide the letters if necessary for the children to choose from and copy.

◆ Using three verbs chosen from the text, such as *sew*, *make* and *glue*, ask the children to make up new instructions for making a toy of their own, such as a bear. Model the writing of these instructions on the board.

The clothes people wore

genre
information
text; labels

In the days when your grandparents were young, people dressed in many different styles. Here are two of those styles:

short hairstyles

large earrings

short collars

plastic-coated material

flower pattern

close fitted suits

short mini-dress

coloured nylon tights

white slip-on shoes

The Hulton Getty Picture Collection

The clothes people wore

Area of study
Changes in children's own lives and the way of life of their family or others around them.

History learning objectives

◆ To place events, people and objects in chronological order (1a).
◆ To use common words and phrases related to the passing of time (1b).
◆ To identify differences between ways of life at different times (2b).
◆ To find out about the past from pictures and text (4a).

Background notes

Children often identify with clothes and fashions in the past more readily than with other aspects of past times and it is through reference to styles of dress that they are most often able to place pictures in the correct period. These pictures illustrate fashion in the 1960s – a period when the children's grandparents might have been young adults. The images therefore provide an opportunity to relate new learning to the lives of the children's own families, making it meaningful and relevant to them. Their older family members may well remember the era of mini-skirts and tight trousers, and may even have photographs of their own from this time. Pictures from other times in the past, and of other present-day pictures, are a useful resource for making comparisons and working on the children's developing sense of the past and of chronology and sequence.

Literacy work can look at the use of captions and labels, which will link with other work using labels around the classroom and in other lessons.

Vocabulary

Mini-dress; suits; slip-on shoes; nylon tights; collars; plastic; earrings.

Discussing the text

◆ Look at the pictures with the children. Read through the captions to and with the children. Ask: *What is this text about?*
◆ Do the children know which people might have dressed like this? Point out that these styles might have been fashionable when their grandparents were young.
◆ What are the words called which tell us the names of the clothes and styles? (For example, labels, captions.)
◆ Why is the woman's dress called *mini*?
◆ Do the children like these fashions? Do they like the flower pattern on the dress and the coloured tights?
◆ Do they see styles like this nowadays? Do their dads wear white shoes? Explain how fashions sometimes come back and we see things again that have 'gone out' of fashion.
◆ What sorts of styles do we see now?
◆ Which is their own favourite style?

History activities

◆ Collect pictures of different types of dress from various times in the past, such as modern, 1960s and 70s, wartime, Edwardian, Victorian, Tudor, and so on. These could be taken from old magazines or from published materials.

Discuss how clothes have changed over the years.

Choose two large pictures – one which is distinctly present-day and one which is obviously from a distant time in the past, such as Victorian. Working with the whole class, place the pictures in sequence, modern and old-fashioned. Ask the children to say how they know that one is from the past. Repeat the activity with three or four pictures, making them less obvious each time.

Give small groups sets of pictures to place in time order. Notice how the children do this and ask them to explain how they made their decisions.

Look at short video clips of period programmes from the television and discuss the styles of dress in these.

Visit a museum that specialises in costume to extend the range of styles the children are familiarised with.

Borrow, or organise the making of, some old-fashioned costumes for use as dressing-up clothes, a structured play area or short plays made up by the children.

Create a 'tableau', in which the children dress and pose in the same attitude as in one of the pictures in the class collection.

◆ Make a large wall chart, divided into general chronological periods and encourage the children to add pictures to it in the correct periods.

Further literacy ideas

Using a large picture of costume from a past time, model with the whole class the placing of labels or captions in appropriate places. Get the children to read the labels.

◆ Photocopy some of the pictures which have been collected onto A4 sheets and provide appropriate words for the children to use as labels. Get the children to label their pictures while working independently.

Alternatively, ask the children to write their own words as labels onto photocopied pictures.

During shared reading time, ask the children about the labels on the pictures. *Why are there no capital letters?*

Give the children large sheets of paper to paste their sequences of pictures on. Ask them to write a comment below each picture, saying why it is in that place in the sequence, or alternatively, describing the clothes in each one.

Tom's first day at school

Genre
*narrative text;
modern fiction*

Tom was very happy because it was his birthday and his first day at school. His mum took him through the big gate, through the big playground with all its swings, into his classroom.

"Marmalade," Tom said (he always said that when he was surprised). "What a lot of things there are to do here!"

There was painting and water and sand, and soft squidgy stuff called clay, all on tables, and a nice teacher with a mini-skirt.

"Hello," she said, "I'm Mrs Maloney."

"Hello," said Tom. "Can I play with all these things?"

The teacher said he could, and while Tom played with everything, his mum talked to the teacher.

"See you later, Tom," said his mum. "I won't forget your birthday present." Tom waved to his mum, but didn't answer because he was too busy looking at the pets in his classroom's pets' corner.

From 'Tom's First Day at School', by Malcolm Carrick, in *Storytime from Play School*

First day at school

A millionbillionwillion miles from home
Waiting for the bell to go. (To go where?)
Why are they all so big, other children?
So noisy? So much at home they
must have been born in uniform
Lived all their lives in playgrounds
Spent the years inventing games
that don't let me in. Games
that are rough, that swallow you up.

And the railings.
All around, the railings.
Are they to keep out wolves and monsters?
Things that carry off and eat children?
Things you don't take sweets from?
Perhaps they're to stop us getting out
Running away from the lessins. Lessin.
What does a lessin look like?
Sounds small and slimy.
They keep them in glassrooms.
Whole rooms made out of glass. Imagine.

I wish I could remember my name
Mummy said it would come in useful.
Like wellies. When there's puddles.
Lellowwellies. I wish she was here.
I think my name is sewn on somewhere
Perhaps the teacher will read it for me.
Tea-cher. The one who makes tea.

by Roger McGough

First day at school

Area of study
Changes in children's own lives and the way of life of their family or others around them.

History learning objectives

◆ To place events, people and objects in chronological order (1a).
◆ To use common words and phrases related to the passing of time (1b).
◆ To recognise why people did things and why events happened… (2a).
◆ To find out about the past from text (4a).

Background notes

Starting school is perhaps the biggest event in the lives of young children. They will probably be able to remember the day that they started school and hopefully they will be able to talk about their own experiences and compare these to the two versions presented here, discussing how they felt and whether they thought they would like school or not. There is the opportunity also for them to attempt to recall in detail what they first saw and what they did. The experiences of the children's parents or carers will provide an additional historical dimension.

These two extracts provide opportunities for differences to be identified. For example, one is a story, while the other is a poem. One presents a happy picture of the first day, while the other finds school strange and rather frightening. There are also numerous differences in style between the two texts. They are quite challenging texts for Key Stage 1, and children will need considerable support in reading and using them. However, the children's understanding of their content will generate interest and help them to meet the challenge.

Vocabulary

First; school; children; play; games; classroom; teacher.

Discussing the text

◆ Read the story and then the poem to and with the class.
◆ Ask the children what the differences are between the two extracts. (For example, one is a story, the other is a poem.)
◆ Ask: *What are these two extracts about?*
◆ Do both the children who are starting school feel the same about it?
◆ Ask: *Why does Tom like his first day? Why does the child in the poem not like it?*
◆ Do the class think that the story and poem were written by children? If not, who do they think wrote them? Ask the children how the authors know what a first day at school is like.
◆ Ask: *What sort of things does Tom, in the story, begin to notice on his first day?*
◆ Ask: *What does the child in the poem notice?*
◆ Do the children think these versions are fact or fiction?
◆ Ask: *Why does the child in the poem think that classrooms are made out of glass, and that the teacher is the one who makes the tea?*
◆ Ask: *Why does the child in the poem think that school is 'a millionbillionwillion' miles from home? Is there really such a word as this? What does it mean?*

Which one did they enjoy better – the story or the poem?

History activities

Ask the children to try to think back to their first day at school. Perhaps tell them about your own memories. Who can remember what happened on that day?

What did they do on their first day? Did they enjoy it or were they a little bit afraid?

Can they remember how old they were? How old are they now?

For homework, ask them to talk to their parents or carers about their memories of school. Can their parents or carers remember their first day at school? (It might also be useful to send a note home about this or to speak directly to parents/carers after school. If possible ask them to send to school some simple sentences about their experiences for the children to read.)

When the children have done this, ask them to tell the class about what they have found out. Were their parents' experiences very different from their own? How has school changed since the days of the older people in their homes?

◆ Ask the children to draw pictures of their first classroom and their first teacher.

Make a wall display or class book of all the writing and pictures that have been collected.

Further literacy ideas

◆ Write the words from the list of vocabulary on the board for the children to read. Get the children to put them into their word books or wordbanks.

While re-reading the story with the class, draw the children's attention to the direct speech and the use of speech marks.

While looking at the poem, note where the sentences begin and end. Ask the children to find the beginnings of new sentences. How do they know where a new sentence begins? In shared writing time, model the writing of some sentences.

Ask the children to draw a picture of a classroom. Model for them how to add boxes for labels. Alternatively, provide them with a picture with space for labels. Ask the children to put the correct words in the boxes, using appropriate words from the list of vocabulary you give them.

◆ Challenge the children to write either a short story or a poem about their own first day at school. Ask them to decide whether they want their writing to be informative, sad or funny.

Going through the old photos

Genre
rhyming poem

Who's that?
That's your Auntie Mabel
and that's me
under the table.

Who's that?
That's Uncle Billy.
Who's that?
Me being silly.

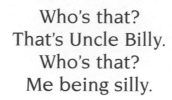

Who's that
licking a lolly?
I'm not sure
but I think it's Polly.

Who's that
Behind the tree?
I don't know,
I can't see.
Could be you.
Could be me.

Who's that?
Baby Joe.
Who's that?
I don't know.

Who's that standing
on his head?
Turn it round.
It's Uncle Ted.

by Michael Rosen

Going through the old photos

Area of study
Changes in children's own lives and the way of life of their family or others around them.

History learning objectives

- To place events, people and objects in chronological order (1a).
- To use common words and phrases related to the passing of time (1b).
- To identify differences between ways of life at different times (2b).
- To identify different ways in which the past is represented (3b).
- To find out about the past from photographs and text (4a).

Background notes

This poem links well with family history and helps build up or reinforce children's prior knowledge and learning about the past, following on from the Foundation Stage. Many activities link with the use of old photos, and through the discussion that takes place, a great deal of time-related vocabulary can be used. The value of family photos is immense; they can stimulate curiosity, interest, questions and conversation. The close link with the children's own lives is a significant motivating force, while at the same time exemplifying for the children in a meaningful way, what is meant by historical evidence and the different ways the past is represented. If there are cultural or religious problems associated with bringing in photos to school, the teacher's own photos, or perhaps photos of the royal family, or another well-known family could be used instead as a stimulus.

There is scope here for a focus on chronology and the language related to the passing of time. Family photographs could be used for sequencing or timeline work, building up a real understanding of chronology and change in the children's minds. Literacy work can focus here on the use of questions, and also of simple rhymes, which alternate in this poem. The use of humour could also be looked at.

Vocabulary

Who; Mabel; table; Billy; silly; lolly; Polly; tree; see; me; Joe; know; head; Ted.

Discussing the text

- Read the poem to and with the class, ensuring that they understand the conversational tone in which it is written.
- ◆ What kind of writing do the children think this is?
- What do they notice about the endings of the lines?
- Can they say where the rhymes are in the text?
- ◆ What special kind of punctuation marks can they see?
- Ask: *Why are so many questions being asked?* Is this what they do when they look at old photos at home? What do the children think is happening in the poem? (For example, a child is looking at the family photos with an adult and asking questions about them.)
- ◆ Who do they think is the narrator in this poem? *Why was s/he 'under the table'? How old was this person when the photos were taken?*
- ◆ Have they got old photo albums? Do they like looking through them?
- ◆ Who do they see in their photos at home? Do they have uncles, aunties, grandmas and grandads in them?
- Have they got photos with their friends in too?

History activities

◆ Bring in a collection of your own photos from home to show the children. Also send out a note or ask the children to ask their families/carers if they could bring in some old family photos to school. Also collect some very old photos from earlier in the last century or, if possible, from Victorian times. Take some present-day photos with a digital camera.

◆ Talk about all the different collections of photos with the class and with groups and individuals. Notice what questions they ask. Write down some of the children's questions as you listen.

◆ Pick out some recent photos, some from the children's parents' generation, some from their grandparents' time and some even older ones, if possible. Working first with the class as a whole, model ways of making sequences of photos according to chronology.

◆ Give selections of photos to small groups for them to sequence. Ask the children why they have sequenced them in a particular order. How do they know which is a newer or an older photo?

◆ With the permission of the owners, make photocopies of some of the photos for a class collection, display or book.

◆ Make a timeline for the wall, marked in decades, and add the photos to their respective decades.

◆ Make some 'family trees' either while working with groups or with the whole class. Use this as an opportunity to talk to the children about relationships in families, for example their dad's dad is called grandad; their mum's sister is their auntie.

◆ If possible, look at the class photo from the previous year. Ask the children to look at themselves. Discuss how they are now a year older. What differences can they see in themselves?

Further literacy ideas

◆ Pick out the rhyming words from the text and write them on the board. Discuss with the class how they rhyme and get the children to re-read them together.

◆ Ask the children to think of other pairs of rhyming words. Add all the words to their word books or wordbanks.

◆ During shared reading time, ask the children to pick out the questions in the text. How do they know which are the questions?

◆ While working in small groups, pairs or individually, ask the children to write short sentences or questions about their favourite photos. Tell them that they must use capital letters, full stops or question marks as appropriate. These could be added as captions to the class timeline.

◆ During shared writing time, compose a class poem, using some of the children's ideas from the above activity. Include some rhymes. Display the class poem along with the photos it was based upon.

◆ Give the children some simple blank outlines for 'family trees', leaving empty boxes for them to insert the words *mother, father, grandma, or grandad*. Small photocopied pictures made from the photos could be pasted alongside the words.

A party

Genre
rhyming
poem

On Willy's birthday, as you see,
These little boys have come to tea.
But, oh! how very sad to tell!
They have not been behaving well.
For ere they took a single bite,
They all began to scold and fight.

The little boy whose name was Ned,
He wanted jelly on his bread;
The little boy whose name was Sam,
He vowed he would have damson jam;
The little boy whose name was Phil
Said, "I'll have honey! Yes – I – WILL!!"

BUT –

The little boy whose name was Paul,
While they were quarrelling, ate it all.

by Laura E Richards

A party

Area of study
Changes in children's own lives and the way of life of their family or others around them.

History learning objectives

◆ To use common words and phrases related to the passing of time (1b).
◆ To identify differences between ways of life at different times (2b).
◆ To identify different ways in which the past is represented (3).
◆ To find out about the past from text (4a).

Background notes

This poem, written in the days when children went to tea to eat jam, or honey, and bread, provides good opportunities for comparison with children's parties now. All young children remember parties and can talk about their own experiences of them. For the young child, this is real, meaningful history.

　　This humorous example gives children the chance to see what parties were like in the days of their parents or grandparents, and to find out what has changed and what has stayed the same. For literacy work, there is a useful focus on rhyme, which is clear and simple in this example. The poem also provides useful examples of sentence punctuation and of the use of the exclamation mark.

Vocabulary

See; tea; tell; well; bite; fight; Ned; bread; Sam; jam; Phil; will; Paul; all.

Discussing the text

◆ Read the poem to and with the children.
◆ Ask the children what kind of text this is.
◆ What do they notice about the end of each line? (A rhyme.)
◆ Can the children say what is happening in the poem? Can they tell what kind of party it is?
◆ Can they name any of the children who are at the party?
◆ Why do the children think that the boys at the party started fighting?
◆ Would they like to be at the party in the poem? Why, or why not?
◆ Do they think this party could happen today or is it an old-fashioned party?
◆ What sort of food was at the party in the poem? Which foods do they think sound old-fashioned? Do they eat damson jam now? Talk about the type of jelly the children are eating in the poem. Do they eat the same things at their parties now or do they have other things?
◆ Do they only have boys or girls at their own parties?
◆ Have they ever had or been to a party when something has gone wrong?

History activities

◆ Can the children remember the last birthday they had? How old were they on this birthday? Did they have a birthday party?
◆ How many birthday parties of their own can they remember?
◆ How old were they at the first one they can remember?
◆ What was their favourite party like?
◆ Hold a small party in school. Make food like that in the poem and also food that the children like nowadays. At the end of the party, ask the children which food they preferred.

◆ Provide materials for the children to draw the party described in the poem.

◆ Ask parents to send in photographs of birthday parties. Make sequence lines with these, according to the dates of the parties.

◆ Provide, if possible, illustrations of parties, feasts or banquets from different times in the past for the children to compare with present-day parties. Discuss with them the things that have stayed the same about parties. Which things have changed?

Further literacy ideas

◆ Ask the children to pick out some pairs of rhyming words from the text. Write these on the board.

◆ Show the class how some words sound the same, but have different spellings. Make a list of these.

◆ Ask the children to find pairs of words which rhyme and have the same spelling.

◆ During shared reading time, point out the use of capital letters in the poem.

◆ Get the children to notice how there is not a full stop at the end of each line, but at the end of each sentence.

◆ Point out the use of the exclamation marks, and discuss their use.

◆ As a shared or guided writing activity, work with the children to write some short verses containing rhymes.

◆ Provide other examples of rhyming poems for the children to recite.

◆ Challenge the more able children to write humorous verses about parties they remember, or about imaginary birthday parties.

A growing tale

Genre
*narrative text;
modern fiction*

There was once a boy called Tim.

He was smaller than his sister Sally and smaller than his brother Billy. He was the smallest person in the house, except the kitten and the canary, and you can't count them.

Tim was so tiny he could only just walk, he could only just talk and he only had one candle on his birthday cake. So you can guess how small he was.

He grew and grew until he was two, he grew and grew until he was three, and he grew and grew and then he was FOUR. And when he was four, Tim was a Great Big Boy. He had four candles on his birthday cake.

Tim was now so BIG, he went to the Nursery School. What do you think of that?

He was still much smaller than his sister Sally, and he was still much smaller than his big brother Billy. For they had grown too!

From *To Read and to Tell* by Norah Montgomerie

A growing tale

Area of study
Changes in children's own lives and the way of life of their family or others around them.

History learning objectives

○ To place events … in chronological order (1a).

○ To use common words and phrases related to the passing of time (1b).

◆ To recognise why people did things and why events happened… (2a).

Background notes

Growing up is an important part of the lives of small children. They are encouraged to notice their size, their age and important milestones, such as their birthdays. Young children will relate to this story, and will be able to talk about their own experiences and memories of growing up, and also changes in the lives of any brothers and sisters. To children at the beginning of Year 1, this *is* history, and probably the only history to which they can fully relate and understand.

This short story about a boy growing up until he is big enough for nursery enables the teacher to focus on children's developing sense of sequence and chronology. Through the story, Tim gradually passes the different ages until he is four. There are opportunities to link the passing of time here with counting, and the extract also provides opportunities to develop children's concepts of sequence and of change over time. It makes an important point for young children to understand, that although Tim is growing, he is not getting bigger than his brother and sister because they are growing up too. Time moves on in the same way for everyone.

The story has a clear beginning and ending, providing good links with literacy objectives. It contains a number of clear main points for children to identify and offers opportunities for them to notice words that are used to link ideas and show sequences, such as *so*, *and then*, *and when*, *now*.

Vocabulary

Once; until; and; then; when; now; still.

Discussing the text

○ Read through the story to and with the class.

○ Ask the class what kind of text they think this is. How do they know?

○ Point out the title to the class. Discuss the first line with the children. Does it remind them of anything? (A fairy tale.)

○ Ask: *How old was Tim at the beginning of the story? How old was he at the end?*

○ Can the children tell how many birthdays Tim has during the story?

○ Ask: *When did Tim finally go to nursery?*

○ *Why did he keep getting older?*

○ Ask: *Why was he smaller than his brother and sister at the beginning of the story?* (Because he is younger than them.)

○ Ask: *Why was he still smaller than his brother and sister at the end of the story?*

○ Ask: *Why does the story say we can't count the kitten and the canary?*

◆ Ask the children to show how small they think Tim was at the beginning of the story.

○ Do the children think Tim *really* was very big at the end of the story?

◆ Why does the story say he is *so BIG*?

◆ Why do they think *BIG* is written in capital letters?

◆ Can they say what happened each time Tim had a new birthday?

History activities

◆ Discuss how Tim keeps getting older as time passes. Ask the children if they think everyone gets older in the same way.

◆ Do they think people always get bigger as they get older? Are you or their parents going to keep on getting bigger and bigger as they get older? Explain how people stop growing when they reach a certain age and how they then become 'grown-ups'. Also explain how some children are small or tall regardless of their age and that children grow at different rates.

◆ Can the children remember when they were one, two, three or four?

◆ What things did they do at those ages?

◆ Ask the children to draw a human 'timeline' of four children, demonstrating Tim's size at each point in his life up to the age of four.

◆ Make a 'growing-up' book. Take a single sheet of paper and cut it diagonally at the top so that it increases in size as you go from left to right. Fold it into four sections, and get the children to draw a picture of Tim at each different age, showing how he grows older and bigger at the same time.

◆ Bring in some of your own photographs to show how you grew up. Make a simple sequence line with them.

◆ Ask the children to bring in photographs of themselves at different ages. Also take a photograph of them as they are now, for comparisons to be made. A digital camera is very useful for this.

◆ Using their photos, make a chart showing them growing up, using arrows to indicate how to move from one photo to the next.

◆ Alternatively, mix up the old and current photos, then see if the children can match the old ones to the right child.

◆ Make a class book of photographs, showing how the class have grown up.

Further literacy ideas

◆ Ask the class to find words in the text which tell us when things happened, for example *once*, *then*, *now*.

◆ Using some of these time-related words from the text, get the children to match them to suitable sentence endings, which have already been printed onto strips of paper.

◆ While reading the text, point out how these words link together the events in the story.

◆ Make up some very short statements together with the class and link them together on the board, using linking words from the key vocabulary.

◆ Ask the children to tell you what the main events are in the story.

◆ Give them these events on strips of paper to sequence and read in the right order.

◆ Ask the children to say or write some sentences of their own, using *then, next, now* and *still*.

◆ Challenge the more able children to write and illustrate their own growing tale.

A royal family tree

Genre
reference text; a chart

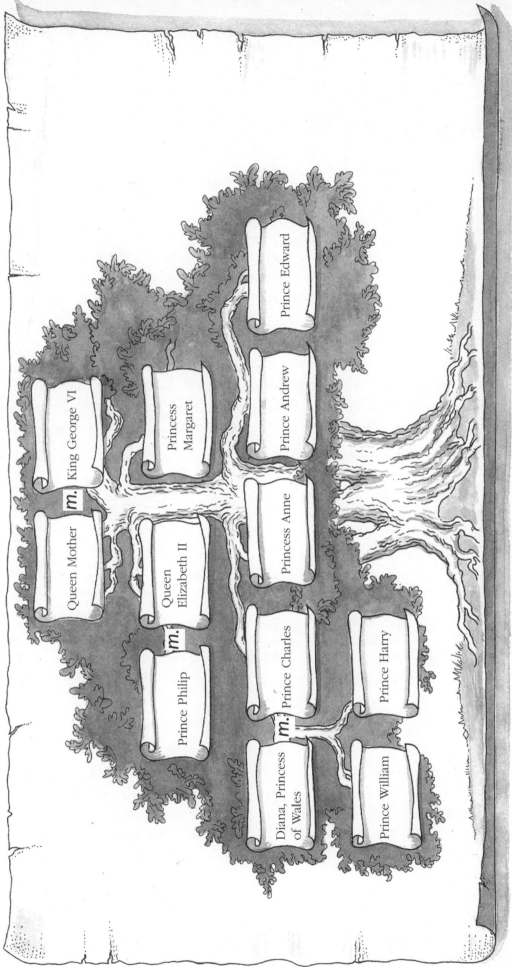

King George VI **m.** Queen Mother

Princess Margaret

Queen Elizabeth II **m.** Prince Philip

Prince Andrew

Princess Anne

Prince Edward

Prince Charles **m.** Diana, Princess of Wales

Prince Harry

Prince William

A royal family tree

Area of study
Changes in children's own lives and the way of life of their family or others around them.

History learning objectives

◆ To place events … in chronological order (1a).
◆ To use common words and phrases related to the passing of time (1b).
◆ To identify different ways in which the past is represented (3).

Background notes

The royal family and news about them are part of everyday life in Britain. Most children, therefore, will have heard of the royal family. This example provides a simplified outline of a royal family tree. It avoids the potential difficulties inherent in relying solely on examples from the children's own families. However, it does provide opportunities to discuss how sometimes children do not have both a mother and father at home, as in the cases of Prince William and Prince Harry. Children from single-parent families will therefore not feel that they are unusual or in any way 'wrong' or inferior.

The chart presents an idea upon which children can build, using their own family relationships as the content. It allows for discussion of issues to do with families, such as the relationships between people, giving greater depth of understanding to terms such as *uncle*, *grandad*, and so on. It makes use of the links with literacy in that it provides an opportunity for reading and producing flow charts that show the relationships within families and the names of these relationships. Charts can be discussed as a different way of interpreting the past.

Vocabulary

King; Queen; Prince; Princess; Queen Mother.

Discussing the text

◆ Read through the captions with the class.
◆ Ask the children: *What could we call this kind of writing?* (A chart or a family tree.)
◆ Ask: *Does it include any sentences? Why not?*
◆ Discuss why a chart like this is very useful for looking things up. For example, it is quick and very simple to read. The boxes and lines help to guide the reader to the information they need.
◆ Ask the children if they can see any other reason for the lines to be there between the boxes. *What is their job in the text?* (They show the relationships between the people they link together.)
◆ Ask the children questions about the relationships in the chart. For example, ask: *Who are the parents of William and Harry? Who is the first son of Elizabeth II? Who is her daughter?*
◆ Discuss how the sons and daughters of kings and queens are called princes and princesses. Have they ever heard of these titles before? Where have they heard them? For example, from fairy tales such as 'The princess and the pea', 'Sleeping Beauty' or 'Cinderella'.

History activities

(For any activity below, if there are sensitive problems in relation to any of the children's families, it might be more suitable to use another famous family or a family tree created from the characters in a book that they are reading, rather than using the children's own families.)

◆ Look at a more extensive royal family tree that shows more about other members of the family, or that goes back further in time. Ask the children to find out answers to questions about the royal family from a larger family tree. For example, who was the Queen's grandfather; who was her great-great grandmother?

◆ Collect pictures of the kings and queens down the ages and put these onto a large family tree.

◆ Ask the children to bring in family photos, or write to their parents/carers with a request to borrow some photos for a time or to use some in the children's work.

◆ Allow the children time to talk about their photos and then see if they can arrange them into a chart of their own. Alternatively ask them to draw pictures of their family members onto a chart.

◆ Make a class book of photographs of family members or other people who live in the children's homes.

◆ Show the class pictures of other famous families, such as the Tudor kings and queens. Arrange these into a family tree. Put this on display.

◆ Give the children pictures and names of the same families as in the display and ask them to arrange them into chronological order, making up their own sequence lines.

Further literacy ideas

◆ Why do nearly all of the words begin with capital letters? Working with the whole class, think of other titles and names and model writing them, beginning with capital letters.

◆ Enlarge one family tree, which one of the children has made, to use with the whole class or with groups. Ask individuals to make statements about the family tree *This is his/her brother. His name is Tom.* Then see if any of the children can change this statement into a question. Model the process first.

◆ Provide the children with a very simple blank chart in the shape of a family tree and ask them to put in any relations that they have. This can, of course, be a very sensitive issue, and if there are children with family problems, perhaps explain to them at this stage that it is quite normal for people not to have a name in every box. In fact it is quite difficult to have the same kind of tree as the royal family!

◆ If it is felt that the above activity is unsuitable, perhaps work with the whole class to complete a chart about another family, such as your own, or one the children know of from a story or TV programme.

CHAPTER 2

Life in the more distant past

One of the few criticisms of history teaching at Key Stage 1 in the past has been the lack of differentiation between different historical periods. Inspectors have found that young children have tended to 'lump' everything together, into 'now' and 'then'. Indeed, to some extent, the curriculum at Key Stage 1 lends itself to this approach with the requirement that children learn about 'the way of life of people *in the more distant past…*' The 'more distant past' has therefore been divided into two sections in this book to allow the teacher greater flexibility in choosing different periods. Chapter 2 looks at the most recent period beyond the living memory of the children and most of their immediate family members, and includes texts written during the previous two centuries, from the early 1800s to the end of the Second World War.

The texts here relate to childhood and enable the children to compare their own lives with the experiences of children in previous centuries. There are texts on games and toys, washday, what was eaten for meals and objects that were used. Early experiences from the childhood of others are recounted, such as in 'Then' where the child poet hears calls and noises in the night, very different from those heard in modern times. After having looked at changes within living memory, these texts enable children to go beyond that time, into the more distant past.

Poetry, rhymes, instructions and reports provide an opportunity to continue to study the key concepts of chronology, sequence and change. They also encourage children to begin looking at texts as sources for the study of the past, in terms of 'what can we learn from these texts about a bygone age?' Children can begin to build up a picture of the way of life of people who lived in more distant times.

The texts allow children to read persuasive, narrative and instruction text in several different forms. There is plenty of opportunity to study rhyme and spelling patterns. More detailed work can be covered on the use of questions, linking words, punctuation and parts of speech such as vowels. Some texts are rhythmic chanting verses, which the children will enjoy learning to repeat, while others are evocative of children's own experiences at times when they were ill or unable to sleep at night. All these things will be readily recognisable to children in the present day.

Genre
rhyming poem

Then

Twenty, forty, sixty, eighty,
A hundred years ago,
All through the night with lantern bright
The watch trudged to and fro.
And little boys tucked snug abed
Would wake from dreams to hear –
"Two o' the morning by the clock,
And the stars a-shining clear!"
Or, when across the chimney-tops
Screamed shrill a North-East gale,
A faint and shaken voice would shout,
"Three! And a storm of hail!"

Walter de la Mare

Then

Area of study
The way of life of people in the more distant past: early Victorian times.

History learning objectives

◆ To place events in chronological order (1a).

◆ To use common words and phrases relating to the passing of time (1b).

◆ To find out about Victorian life from text (4a).

Background notes

The 'watch', or 'watch and ward', was an institution that went back many years in history to medieval times. In the Middle Ages, 'watch and ward' was an obligatory feudal duty that served to protect the community. Similarly, the 'hue and cry' was a communal response to an incident such as theft, where everyone was expected to join in to apprehend the villain. The watch consisted of nightwatchmen who patrolled the streets at night with a dual purpose. Firstly, they marked the time of night by calling out at hourly intervals; secondly, they kept watch while the people were asleep, warding off any wrongdoers. They were like an early type of police force, or vigilante force, whose task was to raise the alarm if necessary. Along with the 'night-soil' men, the 'lamplighters' and the 'knocker-uppers', they formed an important group of workers who supported the community during its sleeping hours.

Here, Walter de la Mare provides us with an evocative image of a lonely man, out in all weathers, still calling out the time whatever the conditions, contrasting effectively with the child, warm in bed. The poem was first published in 1913, as part of a very popular collection which went into many reprints in the first decades of the 20th century. It provides opportunities to look at the language associated with time and chronology, to make links with counting and number, and to study rhyme in verse.

Vocabulary

Twenty; lantern; to and fro; forty; watch; years ago; sixty; o' the morning; hundred; eighty; abed.

Discussing the text

◆ Read the poem with the class. Ask: *What type of text is this? What is it about? Who is listening? What is he listening to?*

◆ Can the children imagine being warm in bed listening to the voice of someone outside in bad weather? What do the children think *the watch* was? How do they know?

◆ Can the children guess why the watchman's voice was *faint and shaken* sometimes?

◆ What do the children think the watchman meant when he shouted *two o' the morning*?

◆ Ask the children to count in tens and then twenties. *Why does the poet count in twenties at the beginning of the poem?* (For example, it creates a good rhythm and it takes the reader back into the past quickly.)

◆ Get the children to notice and mark the rhythm of the poem. Do they think the rhythm could represent anything in the poem? (For example, the trudging of the nightwatchman.)

◆ Talk to the children about nightwatchmen. Ask: *Do we have these now? How do we know what the time is when we wake up at night? What do we hear if we wake up at night?* Some children might be able to hear church bells ring out the time at night.

◆ Can they find any words that rhyme? Ask the class to pick out the words that sound the same.

Can the children see a pattern in the rhymes?

Did they enjoy the poem?

Have they learned anything from it? Ask volunteers to tell the class what they have learned about the past from 'Then'.

Tell the children when the poem was first published. Help them to work backwards from this date to find out when the poem is set. Ask them to think what period in time it is telling us about. (For example, the Victorians.)

How long ago is this time now that it is about 90 years after its publication?

Ask: *What is a lantern?* Have they ever seen one? *Why did the watch need a lantern? Why were the streets dark?*

History activities

Use a simple timeline to illustrate these different times in the past. Discuss how the poem was written in the past, but about another time, even longer ago.

◆ Provide a picture of a lantern, or a real one for the children to look at and discuss. Talk about why lanterns were invented; light a candle and show the class how easily this can blow out. Compare it with the light in a lantern.

After making reference to books about crime and law and order in the past, discuss the idea of 'watch and ward' with the children. On the class timeline, illustrate the sequence of periods in history, from the Middle Ages to the present day. Show how the idea of the 'watch' goes right back to the Middle Ages. Talk about the 'hue and cry', when people were all called upon to chase a thief or villain if he/she was caught stealing.

◆ Make paper lanterns and models of old-fashioned lanterns. Use these as props in role-plays or short scenes about the activities of the 'watch'.

Compare this poem with others about lamplighters, such as 'The Lamplighter', by RL Stevenson.

◆ Provide the children with graphite pencils or charcoal, to draw their own night-time illustrations of lamplighters and the 'watch'.

Further literacy ideas

Give the children the words used in the poem, *twenty, forty, sixty, eighty* and ask them to point out the spelling at the end of each word. What do they notice about it?

Look at all the words for counting in tens. Model the segmenting of the words, particularly pointing out the word ending in each case. Ask the children to work in pairs and write the spelling for the other 'tens', for example *thirty, fifty,* and so on.

During shared reading time, use the children's understanding of the grammar of the sentences in asking them to explain the meaning of words such as *abed* and phrases such as *o' the morning* and *by the clock.*

◆ Notice, during shared reading, the pattern of rhymes in the poem. Ask children to join in with the recurring patterns of rhythm and rhyme.

During shared writing time, invent and write a new example of the pattern, perhaps starting in the same way, for example:

Twenty, forty, sixty, eighty,

A hundred years ago,

All through the night lamplighters crept

Making the lamps aglow.

Working class meals, 1833

Breakfast is generally porridge, bread and milk, lined with flour or oatmeal. On Sunday, a cup of tea and bread and butter.

Dinner on weekdays, potatoes and bacon, and bread, which is generally white. On a Sunday, a little flesh meat; no butter, egg, or pudding.

Supper oatmeal porridge and milk; sometimes potatoes and milk. Sunday, sometimes a little bread and cheese for supper; never have this on weekdays.

Now and then buys eggs when they are as low as a halfpenny apiece, and fries them to bacon. They never taste any other vegetable than potatoes.

Tea-time every day, tea and bread and butter; nothing extra on Sunday at tea.

An extract from a Factory Commission Report, 1833

Working class meals, 1833

History learning objectives

- To use common words and phrases relating to the passing of time (1b).
- To identify differences between ways of life at different times (2b).
- To find out about everyday life in the early 19th century from text (4a).

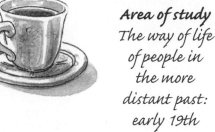

Area of study
The way of life of people in the more distant past: early 19th century.

Background notes

This report is the outcome of a meeting in which Mr Cowell met a Manchester housewife in 1833 and interviewed her about her family affairs. Mr Cowell was carrying out interviews on behalf of the Factory Commission, which at that time was investigating the working and living conditions of the poor in Britain. He comments that he considered her evidence to be a specimen, *somewhat under the average*, of how a working class family lived.

The housewife's husband was a spinner and she had five children. The eldest worked as a 'piecer', and she was paid according to each piece of work she completed for her father. Their combined wages supported the family.

Their house consisted of four rooms, two on each floor. The furniture comprised two beds in the same room, four chairs, one table, boxes for storing clothes, two pans, and a tea kettle. Along with a few other cooking utensils, some cutlery, crockery, and a few books, this constituted their entire belongings.

They subscribed a penny a week for each child to a funeral society for the children. Two of the children went to school for 3 pence a week each, where they were taught reading, but not writing.

The extract lends itself to simple sequencing activities and a study of historical change through making comparisons with present-day family life. It consists of information text and a style of report writing which provides potential for literacy work on the use and making of notes rather than complete sentences.

Vocabulary

Breakfast; tea; potatoes; bread; milk; tea; tea-time; supper; cheese; dinner; flesh meat; porridge; butter; oatmeal; bacon.

Discussing the text

Read through the text to and with the class. Ask the children if they can work out what kind of writing this is. Can they work out who wrote it?

Why do they think it may have been written? Explain to them how some people were worried about the conditions for poor people and were investigating how they lived. These investigations were then reported to Parliament, where the reformers thought that they might be able to influence the Government to improve conditions.

Have they ever seen any other reports? Perhaps they have seen a school report. Discuss what a report is, and how it is used for giving information about an enquiry.

What meals are mentioned? What sorts of food did they eat? What do the children notice about the variety of foods?

Do the children have all these meals? What different foods do they have in their own meals?

◆ Do they have any other things to eat as well as their meals?

◆ What do they like to eat? Would they have liked to live on these meals every day?

◆ Look at the order of the meals in the extract. *What times of day would people have eaten each of these meals?*

History activities

◆ Discuss with the children the things that the family in the extract would have done during the day. Get the children to think of other things that happen through the day. Provide cards listing their daily activities and meals and ask them to put them into chronological order, or to complete a sequence line or chart.

◆ Ask the children to compare the food eaten by working people in the 19th century with the food they eat now. Provide a 'similarities and differences' chart and organise the children to work in pairs to list or draw the two kinds of foods that they have discussed.

◆ Working with the whole class, pick out the major differences between the diet of the poor and present-day diets. (For example, the lack of meat and variety of fresh vegetables in the diet shown in the extract.)

◆ Use the famous extract from Charles Dickens' *Oliver Twist* about gruel, to compare with this diet, whose *oatmeal porridge* was very much the same.

◆ Find a simple recipe for gruel and make some. Let the children try it if they wish!

◆ Using books or the Internet, collect recipes or descriptions of meals from different times in the past, for example Roman meals where doormice were a speciality!

Further literacy ideas

◆ Working with the whole class during shared writing, make a list of the children's favourite foods. Ask the children to pick out from the extract the food that the family described would have eaten. List these foods next to the list of the children's favourite foods.

◆ Pick out comments which are not complete sentences, for example *On Sunday, a cup of tea and bread and butter.* Discuss with the class what words they could add to make this a complete sentence, for example they could insert *the family had…* after the comma. Discuss and explain which words are often missed out when writing in notes.

◆ Model the beginning of a simple report about the meals the children have in the present day. Get the children to work in pairs, individually or as part of a guided writing group, to complete their modern-day reports.

The land of counterpane

Genre
poem from
the past

When I was sick and lay a-bed,
I had two pillows at my head,
And all my toys beside me lay
To keep me happy all the day.

And sometimes for an hour or so
I watched my leaden soldiers go,
With different uniforms and drills,
Among the bed-clothes, through the hills;

And sometimes sent my ships in fleets
All up and down among the sheets;
Or brought my trees and horses out,
And planted cities all about.

I was the giant great and still
That sits upon the pillow-hill,
And sees before him, dale and plain,
The pleasant land of counterpane.

Robert Louis Stevenson

The land of counterpane

Area of study
The way of life of people in the more distant past: Victorian times.

History learning objectives
◆ To identify differences between ways of life at different times (2b).
◆ To identify different ways in which the past is represented (3).
◆ To understand how to find out about the 19th century from text (4a).

Background notes
The Victorian poet Robert Louis Stevenson (1850–94) had fond memories of his own childhood and wrote a considerable number of poems for children of different ages. This poem first appeared in *A Child's Garden of Verses* published in 1885, and calls up an image of a child playing a make-believe game while ill in bed, pretending that the counterpane is a land full of ships and soldiers. The child pretends he is a giant up on the hill made by the pillow.

It is a delightful yet simple piece of verse that provides an example of a straightforward pattern of rhyme that the children will be able to recognise and imitate. While the text opens up opportunities for children to talk about times when they themselves have been ill, and the 'pretend' games they play, there is also an opportunity to compare these experiences with childhood illnesses in the past. Children would normally have been ill for a long time and would have had to stay in bed because the doctors did not have as many medicines as they do now, particularly antibiotics. Also, there were many more diseases that could easily be caught than now, such as tuberculosis and cholera, both of which were extremely dangerous. Children suffered from infections that led to 'fevers' and this meant that they would have sometimes had to stay in bed for several weeks.

The poem is an example of one way in which the past is represented and could be compared with other sources, usch as pictures or prose writing.

Vocabulary
Counterpane; leaden; uniform; drill; fleet; cities; giant; dale; plain.

Discussing the text
◆ Read through the poem to and with the children.
◆ Check that the children understand what is happening in the poem. Ask: *Who is telling us the story? What is the child in the poem doing? What is the matter with him/her? Do we know what has made the child ill and caused them to have to stay in bed?*
◆ Have they ever been so ill that they have had to stay in bed all day? Can they remember what it was like? Were they bored? Would they like to play with toys like this, or would they have other things they could do nowadays?
◆ Why do the children think the poem is called 'The land of counterpane'? Do they know what a *counterpane* is? Discuss how today they might have a duvet on their bed. Can they tell what the *land* is and what is happening in this *land*?
◆ Ask the children to look at the last verse. Can they work out what the child is pretending to be here?
◆ Ask the children what they notice about this poem that is special. They might notice the pattern of rhymes.

Look at the rhymes. Can the children point out which lines end in words that rhyme? Can they describe the pattern they can see in the rhyme?

Read the poem again together with the class.

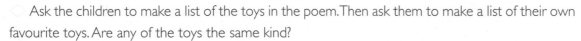

History activities

Make a collection of old toys, such as sailing ships and lead soldiers. (For safety, ensure that you always handle the soldiers, or supervise the children closely when they are looking at them.) Ask the class to bring in one favourite toy each. Make a collection of 'old' and 'new' toys; compare them closely, noting what has changed about them and what has stayed the same. Create a toyshop to display the toys attractively.

Ask the children to make a list of the toys in the poem. Then ask them to make a list of their own favourite toys. Are any of the toys the same kind?

Find examples of old and new versions of the same toy, for example yo-yos, toy soldiers and ships. Use the Internet to find more examples. If possible make pairs of 'old' and 'new' versions of toys. Discuss with the children how these toys have changed. Look at how they are similar and how they are different. Compare the materials they are made from and how they work. Do the children think the use of electricity made a difference to the kind of toys they have?

◆ Discuss what happens if the children are ill. Tell them what it would have been like if they had been ill in the 19th century. Organise a role-play area. First create a 'doctor's surgery' then change the area to a 'sickbed' from the past.

Further literacy ideas

Ask the children to pick out words which they have not heard before, perhaps, such as *counterpane* or *drill*. Get the children to list these words in their wordbanks or word books.

Look at the poem and find how many full stops have been used. How many sentences do the children think make up the poem?

Using the drawings of old and new toys made during the history lesson, get the children to write a descriptive sentence about firstly an old toy and then its new equivalent, pointing out what the differences are.

Ask the children to work in pairs to write about their favourite toys. Model some sentences with the whole class before they begin.

An old Victorian bottle

Genre
report text;
labels

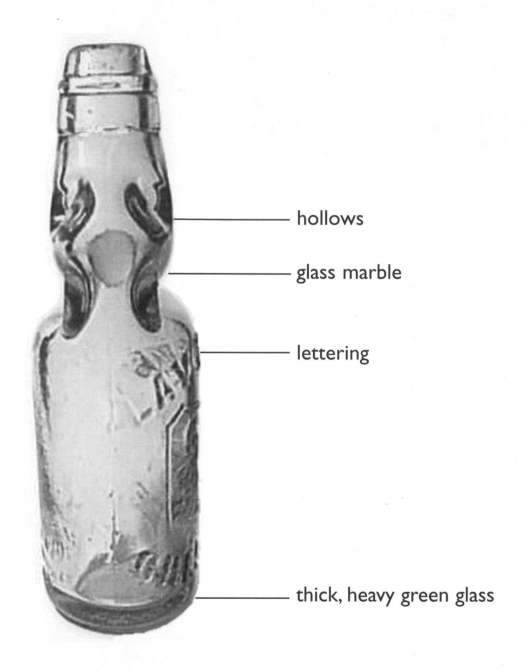

hollows

glass marble

lettering

thick, heavy green glass

This Victorian bottle was used over a hundred years ago to store fizzy drinks. The glass marble in the neck of the bottle kept the drink fizzy. To get the drink out, you gave a sharp tap on the marble to drive it down. The makers of the drink put their name on the side of the bottle.

An old Victorian bottle

Area of study
The way of life
of people in the
more distant
past: Victorian
times.

History learning objectives

◆ To place events in chronological order (1a).

◆ To use common words and phrases relating to the passing of time (1b).

◆ To find out about Victorian life from artefacts and text (4a).

Background notes

This is a bottle of the type made in late Victorian times. The design was invented by Hyram Codd and these bottles were then known as 'Codd bottles'. Just below the neck, resting on indented parts of the bottle there is a glass marble. The indented sides were to prevent the marble from falling to the bottom of the bottle. The bottle was designed to contain fizzy drinks, so that it would be sealed by the marble being forced up into the neck by the pressure from the carbon in the drink. Some bottles were designed to include rubber washers to improve the seal around the top of the neck. To get the drink out, you gave a sharp tap on the marble to drive it down, releasing the drink. Codd bottles are elaborate objects, often made from deep green glass and are very heavy. Lettering is usually moulded into the sides, giving the name of the company which produced the drink and the place of manufacture.

As objects for young children to investigate, they can be a source of great interest and motivation. Children are captivated by the marble; they want to know how it was put in there, how the bottle was made and what it was for. Excellent discussions can arise, as well as the firsthand experience of investigating something so old. There are also opportunities for making comparisons between everyday objects in Victorian times with those used today. There is a close link between literacy and history here, where both require the use of questioning to investigate an artefact.

Vocabulary

Codd bottle; hollows; glass; marble; lettering; indented; stopper; heavy; moulded.

Discussing the text

◆ Discuss with the whole class what the picture shows and read with them the labels and the text in the box below. Ask:

Look at this old bottle.

Does it look like a heavy bottle or a light one? How can you tell?

Can you see the marble inside it? How does it stay at the top of the bottle?

Why was a marble put inside the bottle?

Look at the rest of the bottle. What can you see?

What letters can you see?

What the bottle was used for?

When was it made? Do you think it was a long time, or a very long time ago?

Do we use bottles like this now? Do we have any that are similar?

◆ Discuss how long ago people would not throw away an empty bottle when they had finished with it, as we do today. They would take it back to the shop to be cleaned and refilled. They would get some money back when they did this.

◆ Have the children seen any really old glass marbles? Where might they have come from? Tell them how children in the past would have been given the job of returning the bottles to the shop, but how, instead, they would break the bottle to get the marble out. What do children like to do with marbles?

History activities

Note: *If possible, carry out the following activities with the children prior to reading this text. The firsthand experience will certainly influence and enhance the quality of their responses to pictures and texts. They will also have a clearer understanding of the real differences between new and old artefacts if they are introduced to them in a 'hands-on' way first.*

◆ Provide the children with a collection of old bottles of different kinds including, if possible, one or more of these 'Codd' bottles. They can be obtained quite inexpensively from car boot sales, antique fairs or junk shops. Also provide some modern bottles, made from different materials. A plastic soft drinks bottle would make a good object for comparison.

◆ Ask individuals, pairs, or small groups to put the collection of bottles into chronological sequence. Observe the children's activity, noting how they carry out the sequencing, and how they discuss the task. Note their understanding of the similarities and differences, and their use of language related to the passing of time.

◆ Let the children handle the old bottles and discuss their weight, colour and other qualities. Compare the 'Codd' bottle with the plastic bottle. What similarities and difference do the children notice?

◆ On a simple class timeline, show the present day, and add a label or picture of a modern bottle. Show the children how far back we need to go to put on a picture of a Codd bottle. (Late Victorian times, around 1860.)

◆ Talk about how many ordinary things have changed since Victorian times. Provide other everyday items from the past for the children to handle and talk about, for example an iron or warming pan.

◆ Provide drawing materials, such as soft pencils or pastels for the children to make some observational drawings of their favourite bottles.

◆ Create a 'bottle gallery', displaying the bottles attractively and including labels or pieces of information about them produced as part of the children's literacy work.

◆ Set small groups the task of finding pictures or information about other objects from different times in the past. Encourage the children to find pictures of Viking objects, such as a football. 'Picture base', a software package produced by AVP is a useful resource for pictures like this. Make a display of the children's findings.

Further literacy ideas

◆ Ask the children to identify all the words in the text and among the labels that contain double letters. List these and challenge the children to think of other words containing double letters.

◆ Provide the children with cards to write labels for the class artefact or picture collection. Discuss how labels can be used as part of a display.

◆ Organise the children to work in pairs on the computer to write simple descriptions or informative pieces about items in the collection to add to the display.

◆ On the board, write out some of the questions used when discussing the text. How do we know they are questions? Get the children to think of other questions, and during shared writing time, look at how to punctuate these.

◆ Ask the children to work in pairs with other texts, to find further examples of questions.

A good play

We built a ship upon the stairs
All made of the back-bedroom chairs,
And filled it full of sofa pillows
To go a-sailing on the billows.

We took a saw and several nails,
And water in the nursery pails;
And Tom said, "Let us also take
An apple and a slice of cake";
Which was enough for Tom and me
To go a-sailing on, till tea.

We sailed along for days and days,
And had the very best of plays;
But Tom fell out and hurt his knee,
So there was no one left but me.

Robert Louis Stevenson

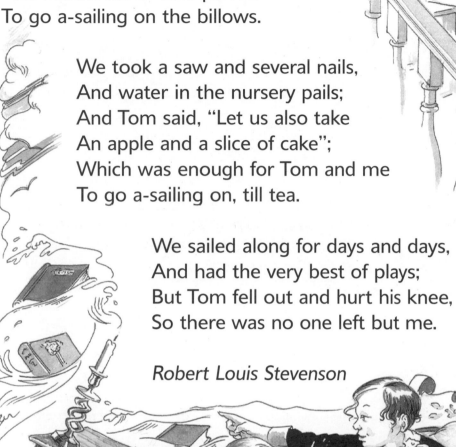

A good play

History objectives

◆ To identify different ways in which the past is represented (3).
◆ To find out about the past from a range of sources, such as text (4a).
◆ To begin to ask and answer questions about the past (4b).

Background notes

This poem by Robert Louis Stevenson calls up an image of children playing a make-believe game, pretending they are out at sea on a ship. It describes how they made their 'ship' and how they planned their voyage. We are told about the provisions they thought they would need to take for the voyage, enough to last them *till tea*. However, there is an apparent contradiction, when in the next line we find they have sailed *for days and days* until Tom falls out and hurts his knee. There are good opportunities here to explore the ways children play, both then and now, and how these games have changed very little. There is also an opportunity to encourage the children to think about concepts of time, how the children imagined they were away for days and days, when in reality it was probably only a few hours – *till tea*. This opens up considerable opportunities for children to develop their thinking about the different ways we see time. The poem also permits discussion of the different ways in which we can find out about the past and how it is represented in many different ways.

Vocabulary

Stairs; knee; chairs; me; pillows; plays; billows; days; nails; pails; take; cake; me; tea.

Discussing the text

◆ Read through the poem with the whole class. Ask individual children to repeat each line after you. Then ask the class to join in with the whole poem.
◆ Ask the children what they think is happening in the poem.
◆ Ask what kind of ship the children are pretending to sail on. (A sailing ship.) Ask them where there are clues that it is a sailing ship.
◆ Ask them if they think it is about today or about children playing a game in the past. How do they know? They might point out old-fashioned words like *go a-sailing*, *billows* or *pails*. Talk about how some words are old and are not often used now.
◆ Ask the children to point the rhymes: *chairs, stairs; pillows, billows* and so on. Ask: *Is the spelling the same for each pair of rhymes? Is the sound the same?*
◆ Can someone point out how the rhymes are organised? (In pairs.)
◆ Do they think the poem has a rhythm; how can they show this? Ask individuals to demonstrate the rhythm as you read a verse.
◆ Read the poem again, then ask the children to join in with a final rendition.
◆ Ask the children if they like the poem. Can they say why or why not?
◆ Repeat the poem on a regular basis over the following days, until the children can all join in.
◆ Talk about the things children imagine when they play; ask the children what their favourite 'pretend' games are.
◆ Point out the difference between the time in the children's game where they are away for *days*

and days and the fact that they are only playing *till tea*. Ask the children why this is written in such a way. *How can this be? Did the children really sail away for several days? What is really happening?* Discuss how time can seem to vary in your imagination; it is not the same as real 'clock' time. Have they imagined things that have taken a long time?

History activities

◆ Discuss the similarities and differences between games now and in Victorian times; do they think that children in Victorian times were probably just like them? What 'pretend' games do they like to play nowadays?

◆ Look at pictures of Victorian toys; compare them with modern toys. What are the differences?

○ Make a collection of different kinds of sources related to childhood in Victorian times, such as a artefacts, books, pictures, prose stories and descriptions. Talk about the different ways in which the past is represented through this variety of historical sources and how we can find out about the past from using all of them.

○ Create a structured play area where children can imagine they are sailing; look at pictures of sailing ships from Victorian times. Talk about what it would have been like on board. Discuss and make a list of the food the children would like to take to sea. Ask the children to draw some sailing ships. Provide pictures of sailing ships from other periods in history, such as Tudor, Viking, Roman and Greek ships. Get the children to sequence them.

○ Ask the children why modern large ships usually do not have sails. How do they move along? Discuss what kind of power made sailing ships move and what kind of power is used in modern ships.

Further literacy ideas

○ Read and spell pairs of words from the poem which have the same spelling, for example *nails, pails; take, cake*.

○ As a class, create lists of words with the same sounds and spellings.

○ Ask the children to pick out pairs of words from the extract that sound the same, but have different spellings. Ask them to make lists of words like these.

○ Find new or unfamiliar words.

◆ Find examples of words that link sentences, for example *which*, *but*, *so*.

○ Working with the whole class, use the children's 'word pairs' to devise some verses with the same rhyming pattern as in the extract.

Genre
narrative text:
action rhyme
from the past

Washday at home

Mother's washing, Mother's washing,
Rub, rub, rub.
Picked up Johnny's little shirt
And threw it in the tub.

Mother's washing, Mother's washing,
Scrub, scrub, scrub.
Picked up Mary's little frock
And threw it in the tub.

Mother's washing, Mother's washing,
Wring, wring, wring.
Picked up Tommy's little coat
And hung it on some string.

Mother's finished, Mother's finished,
Hip hooray!
Now we'll have our clothes all clean
To wear for school today.

Anon

Washday at home

Area of study
Changes in children's own lives and the way of life of their family or others around them: late 19th century to 1950s.

History learning objectives

◆ To place events, people and objects in chronological order (1a).

◆ To use common words and phrases related to the passing of time (1b).

◆ To identify differences between ways of life at different times (2b).

◆ To find out about the past from text (4a).

◆ To communicate their knowledge of history (5).

Background notes

Washday was a hard day for most housewives well into the 20th century. It was not until the 1960s and 70s that working-class families could afford washing machines, and so the washtub and the washing line were common everyday features of life for many people.

This action rhyme is a useful one to use in connection with family history, or a topic on home life in the recent and more distant past. Children can mime the actions, or use the rhyme when acting out washday using domestic artefacts, either from the first part of the 20th century, or from Victorian times. The rhyme depicts activities with which the children can identify.

Vocabulary

Washing; rub; tub; scrub; wring; string; hooray; today.

Discussing the text

◆ Read through the action rhyme to the class and then together with them.

◆ What sort of writing do the children think this is?

◆ Ask: *Who is doing the washing? Why was this? How is she doing the washing?* (By hand.)

◆ Ask the children to find the words that rhyme. *Which lines in each verse rhyme?* Can they see a pattern in them?

◆ Can they see places where the words are repeated? *Is there a pattern in the repetition too?*

◆ Tap out a beat to the poem as the children re-read it. See if they can join in.

◆ Can they think of actions that would fit in with the words? Work out, with the class, a series of actions to imitate the actions described in the verse. Re-read the rhyme together, while the children carry out the actions. Get them to make use of the rhythm in the poem while miming the actions.

◆ Do the children know any other action rhymes?

◆ Discuss how the washing is usually done using a machine today. *Why have things changed?*

◆ Ask how many of the children's mums, dads or carers go out to work. Ask: *Could they have done this in the past? Why not?* What do the children think that mums mostly had to do in the past? Talk about how housework was even harder in the past: there were no convenience foods, no supermarkets, no washing machines and so on. Discuss how women were expected to stay at home and be 'housewives', or they may have been servants who worked in other people's homes. Point out how many now go out to work and how some still like to be at home. Machines have allowed many people to have a choice. Also other people can easily help now using machines, such as dads and even older children.

◆ Ask for volunteers to explain in their own words what is happening in each verse.

◆ Discuss what *rub*, *scrub* and *wring* mean. Demonstrate the actions, perhaps with a scrubbing brush.

History activities

◆ Collect a variety of old washing implements, such as tubs, dolly pins, washboards, wooden pegs, and so on. Use these for discussion, observational drawing and descriptive writing.

◆ Discuss how hard washday must have been in the past. Bring in some heavy linen or thick cotton cloth and discuss how hard it would be to wash and dry by hand. Let the children experiment with this, maybe doing some washing themselves. They could time the washing and see how long it takes, first to wash and then to dry.

◆ Ask the class how long ago they think that the washing would have been done in this way. Make a large sequence line for the wall, marked in centuries or periods of history. Mark on this the periods

in time when washing would have been done by hand. Join all these times together with a 'span', perhaps using coloured thread or ribbon. Mark the period during which we have been able to use machines for doing the washing. Compare the two spans of time and note how short the time has been since we have had washing machines.

◆ Make worksheets containing two large boxes, one for washday 'then' and one for washday 'now'. Set the children the task of drawing pictures of washday, or illustrating a washday implement appropriate to each period.

◆ Create a short dramatic role-play about a housewife's morning in Victorian times, then do the same for the present day.

Further literacy ideas

◆ Using the rhyming words from the poem, look at the spelling patterns. Focus on the word endings and see if the children, working in pairs, can make up new rhyming words, using the same word endings.

◆ Ask the children to point out where each sentence begins and ends. Can they see a pattern? Is there usually a pattern like this in other writing that they have seen? Compare the rhyme with other texts, such as prose.

◆ Either during shared reading time, or when the children are working independently, get them to complete some sentences about their 'now' and 'then' illustrations about washday.

◆ During shared writing time, make up a new verse for the poem.

◆ Ask the children if they know any other action songs or rhymes and perform these. Write out the words to one of these in shared writing time.

An old-fashioned lesson

Genre instruction text; non-fiction from the past

A a

Two songs as in Ada.

Does it sing its long name in apple?

Does it sing its long name in
add, ape, ale,
ace, at, age?

a can sing its own long name
Amy.

A can sing a short song
Alec.

E e Two songs

e can sing its own long name in eel.

e can sing a short song in egg.

Which song does it sing in Ethel,
Edith, Eva, Ellen,
Enid, Edwin, eat?

Bee
Sheep
Edgar in yellow
Edie
Bo-Peep

An old-fashioned lesson

Area of study
The way of life of people in the more distant past: the 1930s.

History learning objectives

◆ To place events and objects in chronological order (1a).
◆ To identify differences between ways of life at different times (2b).
◆ To find out about this time in the past from text. (4a).
◆ To communicate their knowledge of history (5).

Background notes

This example of a reading lesson from the 1930s is an excellent link in its own right between literacy and history. At one and the same time it can be a vehicle for teaching phonics and for teaching about lessons as they used to be in the past. Care will be needed to ensure that the children understand the context and they may need considerable support with reading the names and vocabulary.

Nevertheless, the extract provides practice for the children in reading and responding to questions and makes use of lower and upper case letters. It provides an opportunity to look at vowel sounds and to practise them. It could also be used in its original form as part of a reconstruction or role-play of an old-fashioned series of lessons. It also provides an opening to teach about sequence and change over time. It is a good example of a way of exploiting the links in order to teach both history and literacy.

Vocabulary

Lesson; song; sing; two; name; long; short; add; ape; ale; ace; at; age; eel; egg; eat; bee; sheep.

Discussing the text

◆ Read through the text to and with the class.
◆ Ask the children what they think this kind of text is about and what it is for.
◆ Is it a lesson that they might do today or does it seem old-fashioned? How do the children know that this is an old-fashioned lesson? What are the clues that tell them it is something from the past? (The old-fashioned names; the title of the extract; the picture.)
◆ Ask the children to look at the names used in the text. Do the children have names like these now?
◆ Ask the children if they know all the words. Ask volunteers to point to words they do not understand.
◆ What kind of punctuation marks can they see?
◆ Can the children do the activities and answer the questions?
◆ Can the children explain the difference between *A* and *a*?
◆ The text talks about the letters singing songs. Can the children explain what this means? Ask the children why each letter has two songs it can sing. (Each letter can have a long and short vowel sound.)
◆ Ask the children to point out the words that start with capital letters. Can they say what kind of words these are?
◆ Would the children like to learn to read in this way or from their modern reading books? Ask the children to vote to find out what the class would prefer.

History activities

Discuss how long ago this lesson was written, for example before their grandmothers, and even their grandmothers' mothers were born. Talk about how it was long, long ago, or a very long time ago.

Using the extract and other sources, make two lists of names, those from the 1930s and those popular now.

Make a large wall chart for 'A' and one for 'E'. Make a long pointer and use the charts for recreating an old-fashioned lesson. This could be part of a larger role-play activity, which might include structured play areas on old-fashioned classrooms.

Find other old-fashioned lessons, such as copywriting (handwriting), drill (PE) or an object lesson (learning the definition of an object by heart, for example *A turnip is a root vegetable, spherical in shape…*), to include in the range of activities. These could all be carried out on one day or in one morning, when the children can be encouraged to come to school in old-fashioned clothes, ready for an 'old-fashioned school day'. Rearrange the desks and tables if necessary, to reflect the kind of classroom organisation that was common in the past – in rows, all facing the board.

Create a class alphabet book using illustrations taken from the 1930s.

Look at the illustrations, showing children from the 1930s. Ask: *Have lessons changed very much?*

Further literacy ideas

Working in pairs at the computer, ask the children to find the vowels on the keyboard and try to print them in different fonts, cases and sizes. The printed letters could be displayed and used for further literacy work.

Use the computer to illustrate the vowels, and to change letters into upper and lower case, making use of different fonts and letter sizes. If available, use an electronic whiteboard to demonstrate this.

Discuss the different vowel sounds in *add, at, ape* and *age*. Working in pairs, get the children to think of and, if appropriate, write down a list of words with short and with long vowel sounds at the beginning.

Discuss the use of capital letters in names and at the beginning of sentences; ask the children to find examples of both uses.

Provide the children with large sheets of paper, appropriate pictures and stencils or shapes to draw round, so that they can make their own charts for *i, o* and *u*. They could refer to a selection of alphabet books or simple dictionaries to help them. Encourage them to find examples of each vowel *singing two songs*, for example *open/orange; in/ivy; use/umbrella*.

A message from the King

Genre
persuasive text; non-fiction from the past

8th June, 1946

To-DAY, AS WE CELEBRATE VICTORY, I send this personal message to you and all other boys and girls at school. For you have shared in the hardships and dangers of a total war and you have shared no less in the triumph of the Allied Nations.

I know you will always feel proud to belong to a country which was capable of such supreme effort; proud, too, of parents and elder brothers and sisters who by their courage, endurance and enterprise brought victory. May these qualities be yours as you grow up and join in the common effort to establish among the nations of the world unity and peace.

George R.I.

from The Imperial War Museum

A message from the King

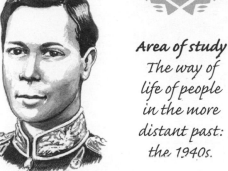

History learning objectives

◆ To place events and objects in chronological order (1a).
◆ To identify differences between ways of life at different times (2b).
◆ To find out about this time in the past from text (4a).

Background notes

It must have been a moment of great excitement for children, teachers and parents when this personal message arrived for the children from the King himself soon after the end of the Second World War. While some of the references will not be understood by present-day children, for example *the Allied Nations*, the letter as a whole provides an opportunity to work on the comprehension of a challenging style of writing, which introduces new ideas and vocabulary. Support and explanation of meanings and difficult vocabulary will be needed.

This letter was written in the first person to children and refers to their immediate family members. As such, young children will be able to relate to it and identify with its contents. It is a firsthand experience for them, bringing them closely in touch with the experiences of children in the war and also with the hopes of their King. There is an opportunity to compare their own experiences at school with those of the children living during and after the war, working on the concepts of similarity and difference, and change. Note: R.I. – Rex Imperator, meaning King and Emperor.

Vocabulary

Celebrate; victory; personal; hardships; total; triumph; Allied Nations; supreme; courage; nations; peace.

Discussing the text

◆ Read through the text first to the class and then with them. They may need extra support with this text, given the vocabulary and style of language used.

 Discuss the kind of writing the children think this is. Ask: *Who wrote this letter and to whom?*

 What was the King's name? How do they know?

 What do they think the children felt like when they received it? Would they be excited to get a letter from a king or queen?

 Can the children guess what the letter is about? Can they guess what *victory* the King is talking about? *Why does he write about 'hardships and dangers'? What has just been happening?* What do the children know about the war?

 Explain to the children which countries fought in the war, and on which side. Discuss the nations that formed the Allies.

 Ask the children to find out from the text why the *Allied Nations* triumphed.

 Ask: *What is the King saying about the children's families? What might the children's elder brothers and sisters have been involved in?*

 Are there any other words in the rest of the letter which the children find hard to understand? Ask them to pick them out. Discuss with the class what they mean.

◆ On a general timeline of British history, show the children the point at which the Second World

War came to an end. Look at the date on this message and discuss how long after the end of the war it was written.

◆ Discuss the King and why he sent a message to all the children. Tell the class about the King's family, how he had two children of his own, and how they had stayed in Britain during the war.

History activities

◆ Collect information about the lives of children during the Second World War. There are accounts of the lives of the evacuees and local information can be found in school log books and local newspapers. Use the Internet to search for further suitable resources.

◆ Ask the children to speak to older family members who may remember the war and then tell the class what they have found out. If possible, arrange for a speaker to talk to the class about their experiences.

◆ Make a class display about children during the war.

◆ Write a letter to the children's families or carers, asking them to lend items they may still have from the war. Add these to the class display, if appropriate.

◆ Look at the gas masks that children had to wear. Ask the children how they look and how they would have felt if they had worn them. (Note: for safety reasons do not allow the children to put on a gas mask.)

◆ Have the children in the class ever received any important messages or letters like this? Get the children to talk about them, or any other messages they have received, or heard of.

◆ Look at video clips or film footage about the end of the war. Discuss VE Day and the street parties that were held. Make a wall frieze showing a street party, with flags and bunting.

Further literacy ideas

◆ Discuss why each word in the phrase *Allied Nations* begins with capital letter. Ask the children to recall the names of the countries who formed the Allies. Write them on the board without their capital letters, and get the children to write them correctly, including their capital letters.

◆ During shared reading time, ask the children to use their understanding of the sentences to work out the meanings of new, or more difficult words.

◆ Model with the whole class the writing of a simple message. Encourage the children, while working in pairs, to think of similar messages that they could write to each other. During a plenary session, ask the children to read out some of their messages. Get them to exchange messages and read those of other children in the class.

Life in the very distant past

This chapter covers a range of diverse periods in the very distant past, which young children might think of as 'very, very long ago'. Ancient civilisations, such as the Celts and Romans are included under this very broad heading and, if teachers feel it appropriate to the ability of their children, they might decide to use the term *ancient* to describe these periods. The early Middle Ages are included, covering the Anglo-Saxons, Vikings and Normans, and also a text from the late Middle Ages in the form of a recipe invented by the cook of King Richard II. The poor and more wealthy citizens of Tudor times are referred to, and a hymn and rhyme are taken from Stuart times when the plague was again taking hold throughout the population.

Although some of the texts in this chapter were not originally written for children, they will be able to identify with or understand the content. Where the original text was far too difficult, it has, where possible, been adapted for greater ease of reading, while at the same time an attempt has been made to retain the style and characteristic features of the original. For example, 'Jumbles' is not only an ancient recipe, but it is still possible to follow it using the modern version here and produce delicious biscuits. Possibly the most difficult of the texts is 'A poor man's property', which contains some Latin as well as Tudor words. However, the content refers to household items, that the children will find easy to identify once they have worked through the initial difficulty with reading the text. 'Ring-a-ring o' roses' is well known to most children. They can perform the rhyme and actions and will enjoy finding out about its past. The harvest hymn is likely to be familiar to many children, who may be surprised to find how long ago it was originally written. Although it has only been possible to provide one or two texts for each period here, it is hoped that teachers themselves will be inspired to search for others. The use of firsthand sources, in the form of texts written at the time has no substitute for providing children with a real sense of the past.

The key historical concepts of chronology, change, use of sources and interpretation are touched upon in the course of using these texts. In addition, the way of life of people in many different times in the past can be glimpsed through these writings, from their illnesses to their homes, food and dress. Several text genres are represented and writing in both the first and third persons is exemplified. There is the opportunity to look at capitalisation, captions, rhyme and rhythm patterns, the form of questions and archaic vocabulary. Above all, the necessity to make use of their knowledge and understanding of grammar to help them decipher the meaning of unusual or archaic words encourages children to work harder at comprehending text, while at the same time helping build their confidence to tackle new and unusual styles of writing.

Exploring a Celtic house

Genre
narrative text; explanation about a Celtic house

My name is Bodroc. I am seven years old and I am a Celtic boy. I live in a house like the one you can see in these pictures. I am going to help you to explore my home.

Look at the first picture of my Celtic house. It has a small entrance to keep out the wind and the rain. The main part of my house, where I live with my family, is round. We use wood to make our houses here, because we live near land that has plenty of trees. We put up tall posts and then we make wooden frames for the walls. We fill up the gaps with wattle and daub to keep out the wind and the rain. We use straw and reeds to cover the roof. We make our roofs very steep so that the rain will run off them quickly and not run into the houses.

Now look at the second picture. Here you can see inside my house. Can you see where we do our cooking? Can you see where we sleep? Our homes are very warm when we have our fire lit. The only problem we have is that it is often quite dark inside.

Exploring a Celtic house

Area of study
The way of life
of people in the
very distant
past: Ancient
Celtic times.

History learning objectives

◆ To use common words and phrases relating to the passing of time (1b).

◆ To identify differences between ways of life at different times (2b).

◆ To find out about this time in the past from text (4a).

Background notes

Ancient Celtic homes in Britain, Spain and Portugal were mostly round, but in other parts of Europe they were often square or oblong. Most of them would have a steeply sloping roof so that the rain would run off quickly. The walls would be built with materials that were readily available locally; wooden in lowland areas or stone in the hills. Where wood was used, poles or planks would be made to create a framework, which was then covered with wattle and daub (interwoven twigs plastered with clay or mud). In Scotland and the Western and Northern Isles, stone brochs were often built for protection against attackers.

This text is written from the point of view of a child of about the same age as the children themselves. It provides information and questions aimed at encouraging the children to observe closely, noticing special features of Celtic homes and the way of life of the people who lived in them. There is the opportunity to compare homes from the ancient past of Britain with modern-day homes, and perhaps to think about how and why our homes have changed. The text allows children to read material written in the first person and to become familiar with instructions and questions.

Vocabulary

Celtic; entrance; posts; frames; wattle and daub; roof; straw; reeds; fire.

Discussing the text

◆ Read the text with the class. Ask:

Who is the narrator or speaker in this writing? How do we know? Which words give us clues about this? What is the narrator's purpose? What is he telling us about?

◆ Can the children say why the word *Celtic* begins with a capital letter? Discuss what it means with the children.

◆ Can the children tell you what materials the boy's family used to make their homes? Explain that the materials used depended on the area the people were living in; homes in the hills where there were fewer trees would have been made of stone.

◆ See if volunteers can identify all the parts of the houses and features of life inside them using the pictures.

◆ What do the children notice about the inside of the house? What do they think about it? Do they think it looks comfortable? Do they think it would have been warm and dry?

◆ Ask the children: *Why does the little boy say it is sometimes dark in his house? Were there any windows to let in light?*

◆ Discuss with the children how the house was made with *wattle and daub*.

History activities

◆ On a simple sequence line or century line, show the class how long ago the Ancient Celts lived in Britain. Mark a span on the sequence line, to show how long the Ancient Celts ruled in Britain (from around 700BC to AD43).

◆ Make a collection of books, pictures, information packs, and Internet resources about the Celts. Find a historical map and show the children where they lived. Ask the children to use the reference materials collected, to find pictures and information about the homes and daily lives of the Ancient Celts.

◆ Ask the children to copy pictures from books, CD-ROMs or the Internet, adding labels and written information from their researching to their pictures.

◆ Organise three groups to research into the lives of men, women and children in Ancient Celtic times. Ask them to make notes, pictures and to put information onto the computer or tape recorder. When they have found their information and recorded it, organise a feedback time when they can talk to the class about what they have found out. As a class, compare the lives of the three groups. Collect the children's work in a class book.

◆ Use the resources to find details of Celtic artefacts, such as jewellery. Provide the children with materials to draw, paint or make models of these artefacts.

◆ Bring into school pictures of modern homes for the children to compare with the pictures they have collected of Celtic ones. Allow time for small groups to work together to talk and make notes about the similarities and differences they can see. Make a class display to show the results of their discussions.

◆ Provide a variety of natural materials, such as twigs, raffia or clay, from which the children can make models or collages of Celtic homes based on the illustrations.

◆ Get the children to act out the work done in and around a Celtic home, for example making the fire, sweeping the floors or kneading the bread.

◆ Discuss with the children what they think life was like in Celtic times. Ask: *Do you think it was very different from today? What was different about it? Would you have liked to lived in Celtic times?*

◆ Create a 'Celtic' role-play area where the children re-enact scenes and activities from daily life in those times.

Further literacy ideas

◆ Get the children to add to their wordbanks any new words specific to the topic of houses and homes that they have learned. Encourage them to use dictionaries to look up the meanings of unfamiliar words.

◆ Ask the children to make labels for the Celtic house using a computer programme, such as *Infant Windowbox* or *Textease*.

◆ During shared reading, point out the grammatical agreements when writing in the first person, such as *I am*, *we live*, *we make*.

◆ Make use of this new vocabulary to write about Celtic homes and compare them with present-day homes.

ROMAN SOLDIERS

Genre
*information
text;
descriptions of
two Roman
soldiers*

Legionary soldier

The legionary was an ordinary foot soldier who fought in the legions. He wore armour plates over the top of a coloured leather tunic for protection in battle. He carried a large shield and a long javelin and wore a short iron sword and a dagger in a sheath hung from a strap which went over his shoulder. He also wore a metal helmet and had sandals on his feet.

Centurion

A centurion was an officer in charge of 80 to 100 men. He wore shin-guards to protect his legs as well as his other armour. He also wore a metal helmet with a crest made of horsehair that ran from side to side so that his men could see him in battle. He carried a heavy sword, a tall shield and a dagger in a sheath.

Area of study
The way of life of people in the very distant past: Roman times.

Roman soldiers

History learning objectives

◆ To use common words and phrases related to the passing of time (1b).

◆ To find out about the past from pictures and text (4a).

◆ To communicate their knowledge of history in a variety of ways (5).

Background notes

Along with officials and merchants, the Romans introduced tens of thousands of soldiers into Britain after their successful invasion of the country. Legionaries were Roman citizens, drawn from the Empire itself. Their numbers were supplemented by auxiliaries, who were not Romans but native peoples of the provinces. The soldiers lived in camps, some of which were built as large permanent fortresses. When the Roman authorities were satisfied that the people in a conquered area had settled down and begun to live peacefully, the army was withdrawn.

This short, but quite challenging text provides opportunities for work on the ancient past in Britain and for developing children's awareness of difference and change over time. The vocabulary involved in looking in detail at the soldiers' costumes and weapons will be new and quite hard for some children; however, it does provide the opportunity for them to begin to build up some subject specific knowledge and the associated vocabulary.

Vocabulary

Legionary; centurion; armour; helmet; shin-guards; shield; sword; dagger; javelin.

Discussing the text

◆ Read the text to and with the children. Ask them what this text is about. *What is its purpose?*

◆ Ask for volunteers to identify the two kinds of Roman soldier referred to in the text.

◆ Have they heard of other types of Roman soldiers? Do they know their names? (For example, *Standard Bearer.*)

◆ Discuss where the soldiers came from and the significance of their name *Roman*. (They were all Roman citizens.)

◆ Ask the children to pick out the names of the pieces of costume of the legionary soldier. Ask for volunteers to point to the appropriate item of clothing and weapons in the picture.

◆ Repeat the exercise with the centurion.

◆ Explain to the children how the centurion got his name. Discuss the meaning of *cent*; explain how it means one hundred in Latin and French.

◆ Talk about the jobs the Roman soldiers had to do, such as guarding forts and fighting invaders. Do the children think they enjoyed being in Britain? How do the children think they might have felt when they first arrived in the cold, wet weather? What is the weather usually like in Rome?

History activities

◆ Using a large map of Europe, ask the children to find Italy and Rome. Discuss how Rome is still an important city today. Ask the children if anyone has been to Italy or to Rome. Show the children pictures of Roman buildings that can still be seen today. Point out how far away Britain is from Rome.

Show the children pictures of Celtic buildings (see page 70) and ask the children to compare them with the Roman buildings.

◆ Look at the great distances travelled by the Roman army. Ask the children how they think the legionary soldiers and the centurions travelled to places like Britain. Talk about the roads the Romans made so that their armies could move around faster by foot. Point out Ancient Roman roads, for example Watling Street, on a map. In a drama or PE lesson, organise the children in groups to march like Roman soldiers.

◆ Use a simple sequence line or century line to show the class how far back Roman times are; explain how the Romans first came to Britain more than 2000 years ago. Mark the time of the Roman occupation (AD43 to AD406) on the sequence line or chart. Perhaps illustrate the span with a small picture of a Roman soldier.

◆ Look at the pictures of the soldiers again. Ask the children if they think the Roman soldiers wore the right clothes for Britain; do they think they changed what they wore? Discuss the leather shoes that have been found at forts on Hadrian's Wall and point out that they wore warm cloaks in cold weather. Make a class collection of pictures, books and Internet resources. Get the children to work in pairs or small groups to find out what costumes were worn by other soldiers, ordinary men, women and children, and important people, such as the Emperors. Encourage the children to record their findings as pictures with labels or descriptions in writing.

◆ Provide the children with pictures of modern soldiers and their weapons to compare with the Roman soldiers. Ask the class to say what has changed and what has stayed the same about the dress of the soldiers and their military equipment. Discuss the way the Roman soldiers fought, for example on foot and by hand. Discuss how modern soldiers use many different types of weapons, tanks, planes and other equipment. Encourage the children to show the similarities and differences they have found and display their work.

◆ Use the computer to word-process a simple class book for the children to collect their pictures, writing and drawings about the Romans in Britain.

◆ Read stories by Rosemary Sutcliff, such as *The Capricorn Bracelet* or *The Eagle of the Ninth*.

◆ Challenge the children to write their own fictitious stories set in Roman times.

◆ If possible, make a class visit to a museum or Roman archaeological site to find further information and to give the children more firsthand experience of the presence of the Romans in Britain. Encourage them to record their observations and report back to their families/carers after the visit.

Further literacy ideas

◆ Ask the children to look again at the word *centurion*. Can they think of other words that begin with *cent-*, for example *cent*, *centimetre* or *centipede*.

◆ Scan in pictures of Roman soldiers and provide the children with an appropriate word-processing programme, such as *Textease*, so that they can use the computer to label the different parts of the soldiers' costumes and weapons. Print these off for display or for inclusion in a class book.

◆ Add the vocabulary related to this topic to the children's wordbanks or word books.

◆ During shared reading, encourage the children to use their knowledge of grammar, along with the clues in the pictures to decipher the meaning of new words.

◆ Make a simple 'similarities and differences' chart, with two columns for children to list these when comparing the Romans with modern-day soldiers. Model the completion of the first few points with the whole class before asking the children to find similarities and differences of their own.

JULIUS WORK CALENDAR

Genre
information
text/captions;
an instruction
maual for
monks

In January we plough the fields.

In February we prune the trees.

In March we dig and sow the seeds.

In April we celebrate Easter and feast.

In May we shear the sheep.

In June we cut the wood.

In July we cut the hay.

In August we harvest the wheat.

In September we hunt the boar.

In October we hunt for birds.

In November we mend the horseshoes.

In December we thresh the wheat and gather up the grain.

Julius Work Calendar

Area of study
The way of life of people in the very distant past: Saxon times.

History learning objectives

◆ To place events in chronological order (1a).

◆ To use common words and phrases relating to the passing of time (1b).

◆ To identify different ways in which the past is represented (3).

◆ To find out about everyday life in Saxon times from pictures and text (4a).

Background notes

The Julius Work Calendar is a Saxon document, rather like a set of instructions for each month of the year. The twelve months are set out on twelve pages, rather like a modern calendar. The images shown here are taken from the bottom of each page. It was written on parchment, which was made from the skin of calf or kid, using thick ink made from oak galls (a type of oak apple) and iron salts mixed with rainwater or vinegar. The book itself is no bigger than a modern calendar that you might hang on the wall and was probably created by a cleric working on manuscripts at Canterbury Cathedral around the year AD1020. It may have been written as an instructional manual for young monks, since it lists the work and holy days to be observed in each month of the year.

The Julius Work Calendar was saved from the destruction of ancient texts during the dissolution of the monasteries in the time of Henry VIII by Sir Robert Cotton, who retrieved it and kept it in his Westminster library. It is now in the British Library.

Clearly, there is an opportunity here to compare an ancient calendar with a modern twelve-page version, with a picture for each month of the year. Children can see that there is a great deal of continuity over a very long period of time, as well as change. They can also learn about the yearly cycle of activities from the delightfully drawn pictures. They can learn the names of the months and also practise their skills in sequencing them. The calendar provides an opportunity to consider different representations of the past. The use of capital letters for names is an obvious focus for literacy work, along with the use of the first person in the narration of events.

Vocabulary

January; February; March; April; May; June; July; August; September; October; November; December; plough; prune; sow; feast; shear; harvest; hunt; mend; thresh.

Discussing the text

◆ Read through the captions with the children. Choose individuals to read each month's caption.

◆ What kind of text do the children think it is? What kind of information does it tell them?

◆ Ask the children to count the number of pictures and statements. Can they think of anything else that there are twelve of?

◆ Ask the children to look at the way the text is organised. Do they recognise the pattern? What does it remind them of? Have they seen anything like this hanging on the wall at home?

◆ Who is giving them the information? The writer was probably a monk. Explain that the calendar is written in the 'first person'.

◆ Can the children point out where any special times in the year or festivals are mentioned?

Go through the months and discuss each picture. Can the children gather further information from the pictures?

◆ Discuss what all the pictures and sentences are about. (The growing and gathering of food.)

Why do the children think that the Saxons had to spend so much of their time making sure they had enough food? Do we have to do the same now? Ask them why things are different now.

History activities

On a general sequence or century line, show the children how long ago Saxon times were. Tell them that this calendar was probably written about 1000 years ago, at the time of the first millennium, AD 1000. Mark the calendar on the sequence line at around AD 1000.

◆ Collect examples of different calendars to compare with the Julius Work Calendar. Compare the Julius Work Calendar with the modern calendar. Notice how each has twelve pictures, one for each month of the year.

◆ Provide the class with materials to make their own calendar pictures, charts or sequence lines using the months of the year.

◆ They could make a list of own activities through the year and create a folding book or a washing line across the classroom, with pictures of their own activities during the twelve months of the year.

Discuss the passing of a year. Do they remember last Christmas? Do they remember going on holiday last summer?

Use resource packs, books, CD-ROMs and the Internet to find other information on the daily life of the Saxons.

◆ Tell the children the story of Alfred the Great, the Saxon King of Wessex, who is said in legend to have burned the cakes. (See *Teaching with Text History ages 7–11*.)

◆ Create a dramatic reconstruction of the Julius Work Calendar, in which the children create 'freeze frames', adopting the poses of the people in the calendar; perform the drama, while children read out the lines to accompany each scene.

Explore the daily lives and work of monks and clerics in Saxon times.

Provide the pictures on separate cards for the children to put into the correct sequence. Observe children working individually or in pairs with sequencing cards and use this as an assessment opportunity.

Further literacy ideas

Working with the whole class, look at the names of the months and work out the number of syllables in each. Ask the children to find the months with the most and the fewest syllables.

Ask the children to point out some of the words that start with capital letters. Ask them for reasons why these words having capital letters.

Working with the whole class, model some new sentences about the first two or three months of the year, describing their own activities during these months, for example *In January we build snowmen*. Then ask the children to write sentences of their own for the others, writing in the first person.

Challenge the children to make their own simple calendars, each month with a caption about their own lives.

Viking place names

Often, the endings of place names tell you that they are from Viking times, like the names on this sign:

-*by* means farm or village. Here are some names and their meanings:

Denby – Danes' village
Derby – animal farm
Ingleby – village of the English
Normanby – village of the Norsemen

-*thwaite* means clearing, meadow or field, as in these examples:
Applethwaite – apple tree clearing
Brackenthwaite – bracken clearing
Braithwaite – broad clearing
Kirkthwaite – church field

-*toft* means homestead, for example:
Bratoft – broad homestead
Nortoft – north homestead
Wigtoft – homestead on the creek

You may have some names like these near where you live, or you may need to look on a map to find some.

Viking place names

Area of study
*The way of life
of people in the
very distant
past: Viking
times.*

History learning objectives

◆ To use common words and phrases related to the passing of time (1b).

   To find out about this time in the past from text. (4a).

◆ To communicate their knowledge of history in a variety of ways (5).

Background notes

For nearly 300 years the Vikings were a powerful influence on Britain. They left their mark on the country in many ways: they founded new market towns, taught the Anglo-Saxons new ways of keeping the laws by organising meetings and councils, and brought with them their own special kind of art. They particularly left their mark on the language – English still has words and place names that have come down from Viking times.

Viking place names are very evident in the North and East, and provide a ready resource in these areas. Other typical endings include *-thorpe*, meaning hamlet or small village, and examples of these endings can be found in names like Burythorpe – hill hamlet; Grassthorpe – grass hamlet; Mablethorpe – Malbert's hamlet; and Scunthorpe – Skuma's hamlet. If you have good readers you may wish to include some of these further examples.

Pupils in other parts of the country will have to rely on maps, photographs and local history guidebooks for evidence and information if they are to cover this topic. Preferably, it would be better to link a study of place names to another historical period if this is more in evidence in particular localities, such as Roman or Saxon place names in other parts of the country.

However they are used, place names are an historical source which has the benefit of putting children immediately in touch with the past. They are one of the clearest direct links with peoples who have lived in the locality at some other time. As such, they have the potential to interest and motivate young children, as well as reinforcing the concept of continuity with the past, which needs to be considered alongside the concept of change. For literacy there is the use of capital letters, and in the examples given here, the use of alphabetical order in reference text.

Vocabulary

Farm; village; homestead; clearing; meadow; field.

Discussing the text

   Read the text to and with the class. What kind of text do the children think this is?

   Explain what the text is about. Have they heard of any of these places?

   How does each name begin? (With a capital letter.)

   Look at the endings of the names, and discuss whether the children have heard of any like these before. They may know some of these places, or they may know other places with similar names.

   How is each list of names organised? (In alphabetical order.)

   Ask the children to say their names. Do any of these end in *-by* or *-thwaite?* If so, point out that their ancestors may have come from a place of that name, which may have had Viking origins. Explain how people were often called Roger of Braithwaite, for example, if they came from that place. This was then later contracted into Roger Braithwaite.

◆ Look at a map of Britain and find where the Vikings settled. This was largely in the north and in East Anglia. Using an enlarged modern map, challenge the children to find with the same endings as those given in the extract.

◆ Discuss how English includes place names from many different languages. Give them some examples, such as names with Latin roots (the ending –*caster* meaning fort, as in Lancaster), or with Saxon roots (the ending –*ham* meaning settlement or homestead as in Horsham and Farnham).

History activities

◆ Using a simple sequence line of British history or a century line, point out the period of the Vikings in Britain.

◆ Look at an historical map of Britain. Where did the Vikings settle?

◆ Organise a short observational walk around the locality. During the walk, get the children to look for place names of streets, squares, or names of special buildings or monuments. Get them to note them down. On returning to school, sort out the names and see if any have Viking origins. Are some of them very modern? Explain how some names may have ancient origins, while others might sound old but may just have been used in recent times to add interest, for example the street names on a modern estate.

◆ Create a role-play situation where children take on the roles of Viking chiefs and elders and work out new names for their area. In their roles, the elders can discuss why they are giving places those names.

◆ Create a simple crossword puzzle where the words are Viking place names, but the clues are their English equivalents, for example *Ingleby*: clue – village of the English. Alternatively, make a simple wordsearch containing Viking place names.

◆ Give the children lists of other types of place names, such as Saxon or Roman. Provide the children with a map of Britain and ask them to find groups of these.

◆ Discuss where the Saxon names are found. Are the Roman names restricted to any particular area?

Further literacy ideas

◆ Give the children some examples of the beginnings of names and ask them to add Viking endings. Get them to explain the meanings of the names they have created, for example *Appleby* meaning apple tree village.

◆ Children can practise the use of capitalisation by writing sentences containing place names. They can then exchange their sentences with a friend to check that the capital letters are correctly used.

◆ Provide the children with a text with all capitals missing. These can be for other words needing capitals as well as place names. Ask the children to rewrite the sentences including the capitals. Encourage the children to write the sentences in a continuous paragraph rather than in lists to provide them with a more realistic experience of using punctuation within text.

◆ During shared writing time, compose some sentences with the class, using the place names given here. Working in pairs, the children can then write some sentences of their own incorporating the names.

◆ Challenge the more able children to write a short story about how a place got its name. They will first need to invent a plausible name.

◆ Play word games, such as 'Hangman', using the place names they have heard of.

The first castles

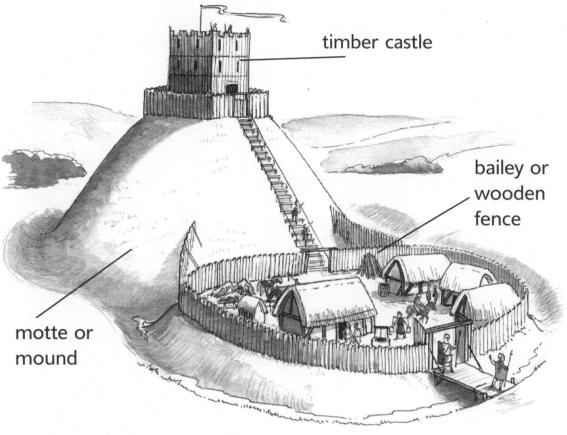

timber castle

bailey or
wooden
fence

motte or
mound

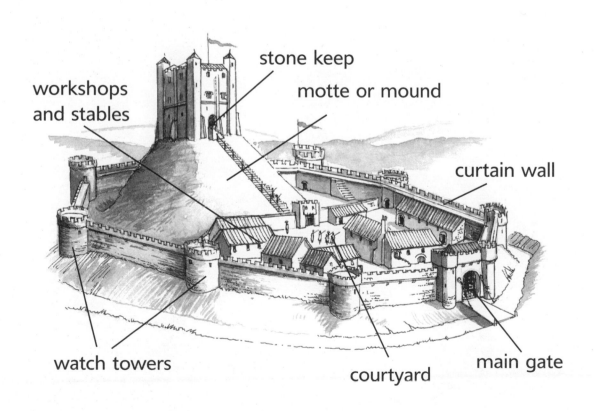

stone keep

motte or mound

workshops
and stables

curtain wall

watch towers

courtyard

main gate

The first castles

Area of study
The way of
life of people
in the very
distant past:
medieval
castles.

History learning objectives

◆ To place events and objects in chronological order (1a).

◆ To identify differences between ways of life at different times (2b).

◆ To identify different ways in which the past is represented (3).

◆ To find out about this time in the past from pictures and text. (4a).

Background notes

Soon after the Conquest of England by William the Conqueror in 1066, the Normans began to build the first 'motte and bailey' castles. After William's violent campaigns and 'harrying of the North', there was considerable resistance to his rule from the defeated Anglo-Saxons. The building of castles in all the main towns was the only way his Norman followers could sleep safely.

As can be seen from the illustrations, the original 'motte and bailey' castles were simple, timber buildings which relied mainly on their position on a hill or artificial mound and a wooden surrounding fence (the bailey) protecting the houses at the bottom to provide enough defence against attackers. Over the years, however, these simple defences were seen as inadequate, and, as the barons and lords accumulated increasing wealth, they were gradually able to replace the early wooden castles with stone keeps and stone walls around the entire perimeter.

Change over time is a key historical concept that can be developed through the study of castle building over a period of time. For ease of comparison, only two types of castle have been included here. However, the developments continued well into the 16th century, and other, later examples could be added to these if appropriate. The various parts of each castle enables children to come into contact with new and unusual words specific to history, broadening their vocabulary.

Vocabulary

Keep; watch; tower; curtain; mound; motte; bailey; stable.

Discussing the text

◆ Ask the children to look carefully at the two pictures. Ask: *What do they show?*

◆ Ask the children to look at the labels and read them, pointing out new or unfamiliar words.

◆ Ask the children to point out all the words which they think were used a long time ago, for example *motte*, *bailey* or *keep*. Do they think we still use any of these words today? (Not often, though they are used by historians.) Discuss how some words, such as *keep* still exist but have different meanings.

◆ Ask if any of the children have heard these words before. If so, when was that, and where were they? (They may have been visiting a castle.)

◆ Have they visited any castles; were they more like the first or the second of the castles in these pictures?

◆ Can they see any other parts of the castles to which they could add labels?

◆ Would they like to live in a castle like one of these? What do they think it would be like?

History activities

○ Allow time for the children to talk freely about any castles they have seen or visited. For those children who may not have had this opportunity, ask if they have seen any castles on television, in films or in story books.

○ Ask the class why they think castles were built. *Who would have built them?*

○ Ask the children to compare the two castles, discussing why they think one is earlier than the other. How do they know? *What are the clues for making this decision?* Point out where wood or stone was used. Point out the additional buildings near the later castle. Do the labels give the children any clues about the castles?

◆ Provide a simple 'century line', a timeline marked in centuries, going back to Roman times. Ask the children to find the year 1000, and then to show roughly where 1066 would be on their line. Mark this place with a small picture of an early castle. Discuss why these castles were built. Tell the children about the Norman conquest and how the invaders had to defend themselves from the people they now ruled.

○ Next, ask the children to count along the century line until they find the place which is one hundred, then two hundred years later. Mark this place with a small drawing of a later, stone-built castle. Discuss why castles began to be built with stone.

◆ Using books, picture sources and the Internet, collect pictures of different castles through the ages. Try to find when these would have been built.

○ Select some of the best examples from different times and add these at appropriate points on the class timeline.

○ There are many castle-making packs and resources on the market. Either use one of these or use boxes, card and paper, to make models. The motte could be made using chicken wire covered with papier mâché or plaster of Paris, which can achieve a good finish for painting. The bailey could be made with matchsticks and the houses and workshops with matchboxes and raffia. Encourage the children to take photographs of the finished models.

○ Challenge the children to find stories and poems about castles, such as 'Sleeping Beauty'.

○ Look at the illustrations in these story books. *Are there castles like those in other books?* Discuss with the children the idea of 'interpretation' and how many different versions can be seen of the same thing.

○ Working in pairs, the children can find out about the people who lived in castles, their daily lives and work, and then report back to the class about their findings.

Further literacy ideas

○ Add words from the past to the children's wordbanks or word books.

○ During shared writing time, compose with the children some simple sentences, using the words from the vocabulary list. Emphasise the use of capital letters and full stops.

◆ Get the children to draw and label other castles which they find from different sources. Alternatively, scan their drawings into the computer and get them to label the parts of their castles using the computer.

Jumbles

Genre
instruction text; a modern version of a medieval recipe

6 oz butter

$\frac{1}{2}$ lb flour

$\frac{1}{2}$ lb caster sugar

$\frac{1}{4}$ pint cream

$\frac{1}{2}$ lb ground almonds

well-beaten whites of 3 eggs

Rub the butter into the flour; stir in the sugar and cream. Add the almonds and gently stir in the fluffy egg whites. Work into a paste. Knead on a floured board, roll out into thin sausages about three inches long and make into S shapes. Bake on greased trays in quite a hot oven for 20 minutes or a little more if they are not set and firm.

These small delicious biscuits were made for King Richard II by his cook. They can be served hot with melted butter and sugar, or cold as biscuits.

Jumbles

Area of study
The way of
life of people
in the very
distant past:
medieval
times.

History learning objectives

◆ To use common words and phrases relating to the passing of time (1b).
◆ To identify differences between ways of life at different times (2b).
◆ To find out about this time in the past from text (4a).

Background notes

Jumbles were made by King Richard II's (1377–99) cook and recorded in a rather incomprehensible recipe in a Tudor recipe book called *The Forme of Cury*. Recipes for jumbles also occur in many later cookery books as they seem to have been an almost essential part of the banquet, following the main feast. In fact they seem to have been no more than a simple almond biscuit, the paste cut out and rolled into intricate shapes – *'Whatever forms you think proper,'* says Richard Dolby. The recipe here suggests that they are made in the form of the letter S but the children could make a variety of shapes, perhaps in the form of other letters of the alphabet. Jumbles make a good addition to festive party food. Orange jumbles can be made by adding two or three teaspoons of finely grated orange rind and a pinch of salt.

This interesting historical text tells us something about the variety of ingredients available during the Middle Ages and the quality of the food eaten by medieval kings. Children will recognise most of the ingredients and will enjoy making the jumbles, as well as tasting them. It provides a list and instructional language with references to past measures that will enrich the children's awareness of changes that have taken place and of the archaic terms that are now falling into disuse.

Vocabulary

Recipe; butter; flour; sugar; cream; almonds; eggs; paste; knead; sausage shapes; lb (pound); oz (ounce).

Discussing the text

◆ Read through the recipe to and with the children.
◆ What kind of writing do the children think this is? What is it telling them to do?
◆ Do they understand what a recipe is?
◆ Explain that this recipe was made many hundreds of years ago for King Richard II.
◆ Can the children find unusual words in the text that they have never heard of before, for example *jumble* or *knead*? Discuss archaic terms and how some words are still in use, while others die out.
◆ Can the children find other things in the text which are unusual, for example the abbreviations *lb* and *oz*. Can they guess what these things meant when cooks were measuring out their ingredients? Explain briefly what the abbreviations stand for and talk about old-fashioned weights. *What do we use to measure out the weight of ingredients now? Does everybody use metric weights?*
◆ Look at the words *ground almonds*. Have they ever seen these? *What are they?* Provide some for the children to see. Discuss cakes and other dishes where ground almonds are still used, for example in curry or the almond icing on a Christmas cake. Make some almond icing for the children to taste.
◆ Ask: *What do the words rub, stir and knead mean in cooking?* Demonstrate these to the class and let them try the actions themselves.

◆ Tell the children briefly about Richard II.

◆ Do the children think that jumbles sound good to eat?

History activities

◆ Provide a simple sequence line – a timeline with the different periods in the past marked on it – going back to Roman times. Ask the children to find the medieval period. If appropriate for the age and ability of the children, discuss and work out how long ago this was.

◆ Provide the ingredients listed in the recipe and make the biscuits. Jumbles could be included in a class party or open day, since they were invented for festive occasions.

◆ Gather together books showing scenes and descriptions of medieval banquets. Using this information, as a class dress up in medieval costumes and role-play a medieval banquet. The jumbles could then be incorporated into the role-play.

◆ Find other recipes from medieval times. (There are a number of medieval recipe books available, or you might like to look at www.foodbooks.com/medieval.htm or www.godecookery.com). Get the children to copy them and illustration them. If appropriate, include them in the banquet.

◆ Collect items similar to medieval tableware for the children to look at, for example goblets, pewter mugs and wooden plates. Discuss how people would have used knives, but there were no forks and people ate with their hands and then washed their hands in finger bowls.

◆ Talk about trenchers or long pieces of bread which were used as plates and make some, perhaps using pieces of baguette.

◆ Talk about how minstrels who played music during banquets and festivals were very popular; listen to some medieval music, such as 'Music of the Middle Ages' by the Sound Alive Consort. Explain how the recorder was a very popular instrument in medieval times, and play some medieval recorder music to the class, for example 'Medieval Dance Music' by the Dufay Collective.

◆ Using books, CD-ROMs and the Internet, gather together pictures of medieval kitchens. You might look at the National Trust and English Heritage websites. Compare these with pictures of modern kitchens, so that the children can notice what has changed and what has stayed the same. Discuss how many people worked in each kitchen. Challenge the children to group the pictures into two sets, 'now' and 'then', and to explain why they have put them into these categories. This can be a useful assessment activity, providing an opportunity to note the children's use of common words and phrases relating to the passing of time.

◆ If possible, visit the site of a medieval castle or house where re-enactments or role-play take place, so that the children can begin to appreciate the context in which these events and everyday occurrences such as cooking took place.

Further literacy ideas

◆ Write the names of the ingredients on the board for the children to read. Ask the children what their favourite things are at parties and what ingredients they think are used to make them. Write the names of these ingredients next to the others. *Are they the same ingredients? What is different?*

◆ Ask the children to pick out the words that are giving instructions about what to do. Make a list of these, then ask the children to think of other instruction words. Challenge them to write some simple instructions, using their words.

◆ Ask the children to write a description of the jumbles that they have seen or made. Get them to describe what they looked like and what they tasted like. How much did they like them?

A Tudor letter

Genre
recount text:
a Tudor letter
(modern
version)

February 15th, 1533

Dear Lord Lisle,

I am writing to let you know that on December 2nd, a ship carrying goods that I had bought sank on the way from Genoa to Savona. The merchants in Lucca can prove that I bought silks for yourself, Lady Lisle and your daughters, as well as for my own wife and daughters. Francis di Bardi can tell you how I paid over 400 crowns for these. These silks and all the other goods I had, galls, alum, cotton and mastic, worth another 200 crowns, are all lost. I wish God had sent it safely, but it is all gone, thank God.

With best wishes,

John Chereton

A Tudor letter

Jesus. Anno 1533 the 15th day February

Right honourable and my good lord, my duty remembered unto your good lordship as your daily poor bedeman, pleaseth your good lordship to know that the second day of December, betwixt Genoa and Savona a ship of Lagos in Portugal that I freighted at Leghorn for to come to Cadiz in Spain, sank in the sea, with as great fortune as ever was seen that any person was saved: wherein, my lord, I lost, as your lordship shall have due proofs of the merchants of Lucca that I bought the silks of for your good lordship and for my good lady, and for my ladies your daughters, and for my Lady's daughters, as much as cost me in presence of Francis di Bardi 400 crowns and above, as he shall certify your lordship; and I never saved the value of a penny, and all the rest of goods that I had. That was to say galls and alum and cotton and mastic, was worth above 200 crowns, and if that God had sent it in safety; and it is all agon, I thank God highly.

And thus Jesus send your good lordship long life, with much honour. Amen.

By your poor servant
John Chereton

A Tudor letter

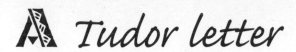

Area of study
The way of life of people in the very distant past: Tudor times.

History learning objectives

- To use common words and phrases relating to the passing of time (1b).
- To identify differences between ways of life at different times (2b).
- To find out about this time in the past from text (4a).
- ◆ To ask and answer questions… (4b).
- To select from their knowledge of history and communicate it in a variety of ways (5).

Background notes

This letter comes from a collection belonging to the Lisle family, known as the Lisle Letters – a useful source for details of everyday life in these times. It is from John Chereton, a merchant known to Lord Lisle, who has been involved in a shipwreck.

The original version is a very difficult text for children to tackle. It is suggested, therefore, that the children read the modern version themselves and then listen to the teacher reading the simplified original. Rather than trying to gain a complete understanding of the original, the children can simply try to work out the meaning of those words and phrases that they recognise from their understanding of what has happened.

The letter provides the opportunity to challenge children to attempt a difficult task. This can have a beneficial effect on children's confidence to tackle difficult texts of other kinds, particularly when they begin to recognise some of the language in it. They may enjoy repeating some of the delightful archaic phrases and learning to understand them.

Vocabulary

Goods; merchant; silks; crowns; galls (oak apples used for making inks and dyes); alum (a type of mineral salt); mastic (gum).

Discussing the text

- Read the modern version of the letter through to and with the class. Discuss what has happened and what part of the world it happened in.
- ◆ Ask: *What has John Chereton lost? Who were all the silks intended for? What had he paid for them? What were 'crowns'?*
- Why do the children think he is concerned about other merchants being able to *prove* that he paid for the silks? (It was probably Lord Lisle's money that he had spent; he may have been afraid Lord Lisle would think he was lying and wanting to keep the money.)
- Look at the original Tudor writing and read it through to the children. Ask what they notice about the style of writing. The might notice that it is very long and wordy. Can they understand any of it?
- Discuss with the class what parts of the original Tudor letter they can understand. Re-read particular sentences to them, discussing their meaning.
- ◆ Look at the beginning of the letter. Explain how letters in those days were expected to begin with a great deal of flattering, flourishing language. Find the point at which John begins to tell what has happened to him.

◆ Pick out unfamiliar words from the modern version, such as *galls*, *alum*, *mastic* and *crowns*, and explain their meanings.

◆ What does John Chereton mean when he writes about *goods*? Can the children work this out from the rest of the sentence?

◆ What are *silks*? Explain if necessary.

◆ Why do the children think that John finishes his letter by saying *thank God* when he has lost all his things in the disaster?

◆ Compare the two endings. How are they different?

◆ Re-read the modern version again. Ask the children which version they enjoyed more and why.

History activities

◆ Look for Genoa (now Genova) on a large map of Europe. Also, on a simple century line, find the date of the event. Brainstorm with the whole class any other key events they know about from Tudor times. The children could make a list of facts they know and then add them to the timeline.

◆ Explain to the children that disasters such as shipwreck and the loss of belongings were fairly commonplace in Tudor times and that it was quite a risky business dealing in goods and transporting them by sea. Gather together resource material about Tudor ships, seafaring and traders for the children to look at. What do the children think life would be like for Tudor sailors?

◆ Provide the children with drawing and reference materials for drawing and modelling Tudor ships. Place the children's creative work against a stormy seascape background.

◆ If possible, take the class to visit a replica of a Tudor ship, such as the *Golden Hinde* at Brixham in Devon.

◆ Collect resources and information about the *Mary Rose*. Look at the kind of objects that have been found that went down with the *Mary Rose*. This is a useful example to compare with the events recounted in John Chereton's letter. The children can draw and label items of interest that they find in these resources.

◆ Make collages of traders and rich merchants, taking care to use appropriate materials, such as natural fibres, rough hessians and cottons for the ordinary traders, and rich velvets and brocades for the richer merchants. If care is taken to make them to the right scale, the collages could be mounted onto a background street scene of shops and Tudor houses.

◆ Provide and read to the class some works of children's fiction about the period. These stories will enrich the children's contextual understanding of the period and also provide the opportunity to discuss the difference between fact and fiction.

◆ Compare the children's findings about merchants with stories about the adventures of Francis Drake. Ask the children whether they think he was more of a merchant or more like a pirate.

Further literacy ideas

◆ Ask the children to identify the words they have never seen before and to try to work out from the rest of the letter what they mean. They can pick out archaic ways of saying things, such as *pleaseth*, *my good lord* and compare these with a modern style of letter writing. Ask them how they would say phrases like these in modern English.

◆ Challenge the children to write one or two sentences using some of the old words they have found.

◆ Ask the children to make notes on the main points in John Chereton's letter.

◆ Get the children to write an adventure story about a merchant who survives a disaster at sea. Model the beginning of the adventure for them before they begin.

A poor man's property

Genre
*information
text;
inventory
from the past*

A true and perfect inventorye of all and singuler the goods and chattells of Thomas Herries in the yeare of our Lord God 1599.

In primis:

Item: one borded bedsted ... ... 3s. 4d.

Item: one mattresse ... ... 1s. 6d.

Item: one downe pillowe and an old cushaigne ... ... 1s. 6d.

Item: two leather pillowes filled with feathers ... ... 3s. 4d.

Item: one payer of shetes... ... ... 2s. 0d.

Item: one bed blanket ... ... 1s. 8d.

Item: one drye barrell ... ... 3d.

Item: 2 salt boxes ... ... 1s. 0d.

Item: one fryer pnn, a pyer of tonges and a rostinge yron ... 1s. 6d.

Item: one litle ketle, a sawer and 3 pewter spoones ... ... 2s. 6d.

Item: 3 little boles ... ... 1s. 0d.

Item: 2 woodinge platters and 5 dishes and twoo erthen potts 8d.

Item: a stone pott ... ... 4d.

Item: 2 stooles ... ... 6d.

Item: a little table and 4 stoles... ... ... 3s. 0d.

Item: 2 old shirtes ... ... 1s. 8d.

Item: 2 old cappes ... ... 3d.

A poor man's property

Area of study
The way of life of people in the very distant past: Tudor times.

History learning objectives

◆ To place events and objects in chronological order (1a).
◆ To use common words and phrases relating to the passing of time (1b).
◆ To identify differences between ways of life at different times (2b).
◆ To find out about this time in the past from pictures and text (4a).

Background notes

This text is an inventory of a poor person's property, written after his death. It was common for this to happen in the case of the poor in Tudor times, since they had neither the knowledge or the funds to have a will drawn up before they died, as was the case with their better-off peers. This inventory gives an impression of what might have made up a poor man's possessions at the end of the 16th century. The labourer concerned was more fortunate than most, for he did at least have some property to leave.

The text is an interesting one because, while the spelling is very erratic, many of the items listed are recognisable to us. Although challenging for young children, with teacher support they can begin to understand what things poor people had in their houses. The comparison of everyday household items will be meaningful to them and will provide a good opportunity to work on their concepts of continuity and change over a long period of time.

The archaic language and spellings provide opportunities for comparison with the present, as well as being a rich source for work on spelling in the Literacy Hour. The children may be interested to know that there were no set rules for spelling at this time. There is also an opportunity to look at the way lists can be written and to see some simple Latin words, which were still widely used in Tudor documents, as well as being in use in the present day.

Vocabulary

Property; bedstead; mattress; pillow; cushion; sheets; pair; kettle; spoons; pots; stools; shirts; caps.

Discussing the text

◆ Read through the text both to, and with, the class.
◆ Ask the children what this text looks like or reminds them of. (A list.)
◆ Can they work out what it is a list of?
◆ Can anyone tell you what *property* means?
◆ How do the children know that this man was poor? What clues in the text suggest this to them?
◆ Look at the words used to describe the things that were found in his house in the list. Can they recognise them? How are they different from words we use today?
◆ Pick out some of the more unusual spellings and write them on the board, for example *mattresse, pillowe, spoone, pott, cappe*. Write their modern equivalents on the board and ask the children to spot the differences.
◆ Discuss what kind of furniture Thomas had. *Was it very elaborate or very simple, for example were there any comfortable chairs?*

◆ Look at the clothes that were listed. How many items of clothes did he have?

Ask the children to imagine and explain what they think life was like for Thomas.

◆ Ask for volunteers to read, or try to read, one line of the inventory each.

History activities

Discuss when this inventory was made and find the end of the 16th century on a century timeline or a sequence line showing the periods in the history of Britain. Mark on the span of time during which the Tudors were on the throne of England (1485–1603).

Collect from resource packs, books, CD-ROMs and the Internet, pictures of Tudor household objects, such as those referred to in the text. Also collect pictures of present-day items from magazines. Compare and discuss household items, then and now, using the pictures, or artefacts and replicas if available. Ask the children what they think has changed and what has stayed the same about the things we use at home.

As an assessment opportunity, give the children the pictures to put into two groups, 'long ago' and 'now'. Observe and note what the children say and do as they sort out the pictures. Note whether they are using words and phrases relating to the passing of time.

Ask the children to make observational drawings of the old objects and write descriptions for display, including the old-fashioned spellings for their names.

Find from resource packs, books, CD-ROMs and the Internet, pictures of Tudor houses, showing kitchens, living rooms and bedrooms. Compare these with the children's homes, looking at what has changed and what has stayed the same. Get the children to share their observations with the class.

◆ Point out to the children that, just as now, some people were rich while others were poor. Some of the houses they see will therefore be very grand, while others will be small cottages.

◆ Make models of Tudor houses and cottages, noting the differences in style and building materials.

If there is a Tudor house or museum reconstruction nearby, arrange a visit so that the children can gain a more complete idea of what home life was like at that time.

Provide a variety of media for children to draw or paint their idea of what Thomas' house might have been like inside.

Scan the children's pictures into a word-processing programme so that they can add their writing.

Further literacy ideas

Look again at the words from the past which had different spellings, such as those with an -e added at the end, or with the final letter doubled.

Give the children some simple words, for example *chair*, *cup* or *fork*, and ask them to turn them into 'Tudor' spellings, for example *chairre*, *cupp*, *forkke*.

Get the children to type in the Tudor versions of some words on the computer and see how the word-processing software underlines them. Discuss why it does this and see if the underlining disappears if the children are able to correct the spellings into modern English.

During the shared reading session, discuss whether there are any complete sentences in the text. Ask: *Why are sentences not needed in the list of items?*

Ask the children to write short sentences about household items from the past and their equivalents from the present day, explaining what has changed.

Ask the children to word-process stories of their own about the life of Thomas, to accompany their drawings on the computer.

Ring-a-ring o' roses

Genre
*rhyming
poem; an
action rhyme
from the past*

Ring-a-ring o' roses
A pocket full of
posies
Atishoo, atishoo,
We all fall down.

Anon

Ring-a-ring o' roses

Area of study
The way of life of people in the very distant past.

History learning objectives

◆ To place events and objects in chronological order (1a).

◆ To identify differences between ways of life at different times (2b).

◆ To find out about this time in the past from text (4a).

Background notes

One interpretation of this well-known children's nursery rhyme serves as a reminder of the bubonic plague. There were outbreaks of the plague in Europe, including the British Isles, for many centuries. Bubonic plague seldom left Britain but serious outbreaks are well known: a severe epidemic is recorded in 446; the Black Death struck in 1348, killing one third of the entire population; and a third famous outbreak was that known as the Great Plague of 1665. After the Great Fire of London, however, the plague never came back to the new London, nor to the rest of Britain.

A different interpretation suggests that the rhyme is much more recent, that it is, in fact, a 19th-century dance. The *posies* are simply bunches of flowers carried in pockets, and that *we all fall down* refers to the curtsies of the girls and the bows of the boys at the end of the dance.

Though the rhyme is short, there is a lot to discuss in it and children will enjoy carrying out the actions involved. There is much historical allusion, which lends itself to the development of activities linked with other curriculum areas, such as art and craft, in the making of posies. There is an opportunity to explore both meaning and rhyme in relation to work in literacy.

Vocabulary

Roses; posies; atishoo.

Discussing the text

◆ Sing the rhyme together as a class.

◆ Ask the children how many of them already know the rhyme and the tune and dance that goes with it. Ask one small group of children to hold hands in a circle. Encourage them to sing the song, dancing round and carrying out the actions described in the verse. The rest of the class could take turns to dance in groups while the others sing along with them and watch.

◆ Ask them to say what they think the song is about. Explain that one idea is that it was made up to describe a very serious illness called the plague. Have they ever heard of this before?

◆ Talk about each line in the rhyme, explaining its meaning:

The ring o' roses is a reference to the rash that appeared on the skin with the onset of plague.

A pocket full of posies refers to the flowers and herbs carried in the hope of warding off the plague.

Atishoo, atishoo is the sneezing which was one of the early signs of the disease.

We all fall down probably refers to the fact that if you caught the plague, the next thing was to fall fall down dead.

◆ Had they ever wondered why they all had to fall down at the end?

◆ Explain that there is another interpretation of the rhyme that suggests it was a dance from the

19th century. (See Background notes above.)

◆ Ask the children why it is called a rhyme. Which words can they see which rhyme? Write these on the board, noting how the spelling of the rhyming words is not exactly the same.

◆ Perform the rhyme once more, as a whole class if circumstances permit.

History activities

◆ Tell the children about the terrible illnesses that people caught in the past, particularly the plague. Tell the story of the Great Fire of London, and explain how the plague never came back after the fire. Explain that we do not catch the plague any more because it has been wiped out through modern medicines.

◆ Discuss how the plague was spread by crowded, dirty streets and by rats.

◆ On a simple century timeline, mark the date of the Great Plague, in 1666. Also mark on the date of the Black Death, in 1348. Ask the children if they think Black Death is a good name for the plague. Ask them to think of ways of describing in their own words how long ago all this happened, for example *long, long ago*.

◆ Tell the class the story of Eyam, in Derbyshire, otherwise known as the 'plague village'. Has anyone heard of this place before, or been to visit it? Explain how the people decided to stay in Eyam and risk their own death from the plague, rather than leave and spread the disease to other towns and villages. Discuss how brave and sensible the people of Eyam were.

◆ Find Eyam on a map of Britain. If possible, arrange a class visit to the village, where they will be able to see the first cottage where the plague broke out, and the grave of the rector's wife, who refused to leave the village, and stayed to care for the people who were ill with the disease.

◆ Collect books and other resources about the plague and Eyam. Look on the Internet for further information. Give the children specific questions to answer based on their resources. Organise a time for them to share their findings with the class.

◆ Make posies in different flowers, herbs and materials. Discuss with the class why people at that time thought this would protect them from the plague. (They thought that good smells would protect them from the bad smells that caused sickness.) Point out how girls carried posies in more recent times as well.

◆ Compare their behaviour with what modern people do when they are ill. What does the doctor give someone who has a bad disease?

◆ Look at pictures of costume, houses and transport in the Stuart period. Discuss the similarities and differences between life now and life during the Great Plague. *Are there features of modern life which help prevent the plague from spreading?* (For example, modern medicines, clean streets and control of pests such as rats.)

Further literacy ideas

◆ Challenge the children to think of other words that rhyme with *roses*. Word-process and print these out for the children to arrange into rhyming groups.

◆ Make up lines to rhyme with *ring-a-ring o' roses* and use these lines to create a new verses. Sing these new verses in addition to the original.

◆ Working in pairs, ask the children to complete a 'similarities and differences' chart, writing short phrases to describe what people did long ago about diseases and what we do now to try to prevent them.

◆ Challenge the more able children to write the story of Eyam or the Great Fire of London.

A harvest hymn

Genre
*rhyming poem;
a hymn from
the past*

We plough the fields and scatter
The good seed on the land,
But it is fed and watered
By God's almighty hand;
He sends the snow in winter,
The warmth to swell the grain,
The breezes and the sunshine
And soft refreshing rain.
All good gifts around us
Are sent from heaven above;
Then thank the Lord,
O thank the Lord,
For all his love.

Matthias Claudius 1740-1815
Translated by Jane Montgomery Campbell 1817-78

A harvest hymn

Area of study
The way of life of people in the very distant past: the 18th century.

History learning objectives

◆ To identify differences between ways of life at different times (2b).
◆ To identify different ways in which the past is represented (3).
◆ To find out about this time in the past from text (4a).

Background notes

This well-known hymn is often sung in schools at harvest time. Written long ago, it is useful for informing us now about the farming methods and the extent of farmers' dependence upon the weather in those days. Ploughing would have been very hard, labour-intensive work, using hand ploughs and teams of horses; sowing the seed would probably have been done by hand, as would the very heavy work of harvesting in the crops at the end of the summer.

The hymn also provides an opportunity to look at how people in the past looked to God as a provider. It creates an opportunity to think about the different attitudes and beliefs of people in Britain in the past, compared with modern times when our great faith is in technology. At the same time, there is an opportunity to consider how words such as *God* and *Lord* would have been written, always with a capital letter. The hymn is written in simple language, with a clear rhyming pattern that the children may find easy to identify.

Vocabulary

Hymn; harvest; plough; scatter; almighty; grain; heaven; Lord.

Discussing the text

◆ Read through the hymn to and with the class. Talk with the class about the kind of writing this is; how it is organised on the page, and how it rhymes.
◆ Explain that it is a hymn. Do they know what a hymn is? Ask the children: *Who has heard it before? Do you already know the words? Do you know the tune?* Sing it with them if they know the tune.
◆ Go through each line with the children. Ask for volunteers to describe what is happening in each line. What is the poet saying? (That the farmers work hard, but it is God who provides the conditions for the crops to grow.)
◆ What special time of year do the children think the hymn was written for?
◆ What do the children think the writer means when he says the seed is fed and watered by God's almighty hand? Ask: *Why does the writer say that all our gifts are sent from heaven?*
◆ Can the children say how warmth swells the grain?
◆ What do the children think the writer of the hymn is persuading us to do at the end?
◆ Ask the children to guess how long ago the hymn was written. Point out the date when it was written and explain how far back in the past the hymn goes.

History activities

◆ On a simple sequence line, showing the different periods in the past. Show the children the 18th century. Perhaps find a picture of ploughing and harvesting by hand and put these on the sequence line.

◆ Use the Internet or CD-ROMs to search for pictures of old-fashioned farming methods and for modern ones, showing machines such as combine harvesters. Use these pictures for displays about the harvest, then and now.

◆ Search for pictures of people dressed for farming work in the distant past. Talk about the kinds of work they had to do. Make rough farming costumes for the children to wear.

◆ Produce and practise actions to accompany the words of the hymn. Children could re-enact the actions of ploughing, sowing the seed, and cutting down the crops with scythes, while dressed in their old-fashioned farming clothes. A role-play of this kind could be used as part of a harvest festival service in school.

◆ Bring to school some examples of different seeds and grains for the children to look at. Talk about how wheat and other grains are used for making bread. Provide the children with pestles and mortars or rough stones and ask the children to grind the grain. Ensure that the equipment is handled safely. Demonstrate how to use it and monitor carefully.

◆ Set aside part of a lesson for breadmaking. Show the children how to mix and knead the dough, let them take a turn at kneading (after carefully washing their hands); then get the cook to bake the bread if there is no cooker set aside for classroom use. Once the bread is cooled, let the children try it. (Check for any food allergies.)

◆ Discuss what the farm workers might have eaten with the bread, for example cheese, butter or ham. It is also possible to make a small amount of butter by getting the children to take turns at shaking a jar containing some very rich full cream milk. They can then put their own butter on their bread.

Talk about people's attitudes towards religion long ago, pointing out how it was commonly believed, as it is by some people now, that everything that happened was brought about by God or the will of God. Using books and the Internet, search for other old hymns to see if the same ideas can be found in them.

Compare these attitudes with those held by many in the present day; discuss how there have been changes in many people's ideas. *What do most farmers rely on now for the safe harvesting of their crops?* (For example, combine harvesters, weather forecasts.) Point out how the weather is still very important.

Further literacy ideas

Re-read the hymn and ask the children to identify the words that rhyme. Make a list of the pairs of rhyming words. Notice how their spellings are the same in each pair, for example *land, hand, grain, rain*.

◆ Point out words with 'silent' letters or letters which are not sounded, such as *hymn, plough, mighty*. Ask the children to identify the letters that are not sounded. Write on the board other similar words, such as *lamb, night* and get the children to find the 'silent' letters.

During shared reading time, ask the children to point out each complete sentence in the hymn, noticing how these carry on from line to line. Point out how there is not a full stop at the end of each line. Discuss why there is a capital letter at the beginning of each line.

Working in pairs, the children can attempt to write rhymes of their own about harvest time in the very distant past. Model the writing of one pair of rhyming lines with the whole class first.

Allow time for the children to word-process their rhyming couplets, and if possible, scan in pictures of old-fashioned farming methods to accompany the rhymes.

CHAPTER 4

The lives of significant men and women

The texts included in this chapter are written by or about significant individuals from Britain Isles and from other parts of the world with which many children will have links. These are people who have made a contribution to either their local or national communities, or to another sphere of activity, such as music or history. In addition to people from other cultures, I have also tried to ensure an adequate representation of women and children in the sample. This is very important, since young children are highly susceptible to the influences and information they receive at this initial stage in their learning.

I have also tried to include people from different walks of life and backgrounds. One character is an ordinary girl, while another is a world-famous composer. Some, like Nelson, were household names for over a century, while others, like Mary Seacole, have rarely entered the history books. Some, like Gerald of Wales, may be well known mainly in their own country, yet their contribution to history is such that they merit inclusion in the curriculum. In short, a variety of people have been included for very many different reasons. As in the previous chapter, it is hoped that teachers will be encouraged by reading these texts to search for other writings by or about people who have made some contribution to history in their own individual way. Indeed, children themselves will think of a completely different set of people whom they see as significant, and these could be added to the list.

Although focusing on individuals, each text will need to be placed by the teacher within its historical and geographical context. Some of the texts relate closely to children's own experiences, such as the story of Horatio Nelson, who got lost as a child, or of Mary Seacole, who practised nursing on her doll. Others deal with more adult matters, and may be found more challenging by the children. More detailed background information has been provided so the teacher can familiarise the children with the historical context and help them to comprehend the extracts more easily in these cases. Each of the major historical concepts is touched upon and there is a range of opportunities to address important aspects of work in literacy, such as identifying fact and fiction, the use of newspaper layouts and sequential relationships in story.

Life in Wales, by Gerald of Wales

Genre
recount text;
a modern
translation of
descriptive
writing from
the late
middle ages

In Wales no one begs. Everyone's home is open to all. For the Welsh, generosity and hospitality are the greatest of all virtues. They very much enjoy welcoming others to their homes. When you travel there is no question of you asking for a place to stay or of their offering it: you just march into a house and hand over your weapons to the person in charge.

They give you water so that you may wash your feet and that means that you are a guest. With these people the offering of water in which to wash one's feet is an invitation to stay.

Guests who arrive early in the day are entertained until nightfall by girls who play to them on the harp. In every house there are young women waiting to play the harp for you, and there is certainly no lack of harps. In every Welsh family the mensfolk consider playing on the harp to be the greatest of all skills.

When night falls and no more guests are expected, the evening meal is prepared. You must not expect a variety of dishes from a Welsh kitchen, and there are no spicy titbits to try. In a Welsh house there are no tables, no tablecloths and no napkins. You sit down in threes and they put the food in front of you, all together, on a single large trencher containing enough for three, resting on rushes and green grass. Sometimes they serve the main dish on bread, rolled out large and thin, and baked fresh each day.

The whole family waits upon the guests, and the host and hostess stand there making sure that everything is being attended to. They themselves do not eat until everyone else has finished.

Life in Wales, by Gerald of Wales

History learning objectives

◆ To use common words and phrases related to the passing of time (1b).

◆ To identify differences between ways of life at different times (2b).

◆ To find out about the past from pictures and text (4a).

◆ To select from their knowledge of history and communicate it in a variety of ways (5).

Background notes

Gerald of Wales was born in about 1145 at Manorbier Castle, Pembrokeshire, the son of a Norman knight and grandson of the famous Welsh Princess Nest. His was a prestigious family, which had connections with royalty and the aristocracy. From his early youth, Gerald was encouraged by his father to become a churchman and as soon as he was old enough to leave his home at Manorbier, he was sent to study at a Benedictine Abbey in Gloucester. In his late teens and twenties he spent some time living in Paris and on his return he was immediately given benefices (a position and living as a priest) in both England and Wales.

He was a prolific writer and historian and it is from his work that we learn much of what is known about 12th-century Wales and Ireland. *The Description of Wales* was written at about the same time as his *Journey through Wales*, around 1190. Gerald travelled through Wales on a mission to gain support and to recruit volunteers willing to join the forces leaving for the Third Crusade. He was most successful in this, encouraging many to 'take the Cross'. In the course of his travels, he learned much about the lifestyle of ordinary Welsh people, which is the subject of this extract.

The customs and habits described here give children a detailed picture of the treatment of visitors and of mealtimes in simple households during the 12th century. The firsthand experience of Gerald comes through clearly in his description. Children will enjoy comparing these customs with their own present-day way of life and expectations in the same circumstances, developing their understanding of continuity and change. This translation in modern English is straightforward and there are few archaic words. There is an opportunity to look at how text is divided into paragraphs, and to identify the main point in each paragraph. The text, a primary source, is an example of non-fiction written in a time very remote from the children's own understanding and experience, while on the other hand, its subject matter will be quite familiar to them.

Vocabulary

Beg; generosity; hospitality; virtue; weapons; guest; harp; trencher; rushes; host; hostess.

Discussing the text

◆ Scan over the whole text with the class before reading it, noting the date when it was written, the title and the author. Discuss how it was written a very long time ago.

◆ Using the brief information in the Background notes, explain a little about the context of the text, for example how Gerald came to write it during his travels in Wales.

◆ Read through the text to the children and then with them.

◆ Ask the children who wrote the text. Ask: *What is he using the text for?* (To give information.)

◆ Ask the children what Gerald thought of the Welsh, judging by this text. *Did he seem to like them?*

Can the children guess why this was? (For example, Gerald was born in Wales himself and many of his family were Welsh.)

◆ Do the children think Gerald might have been exaggerating? Why?

◆ Ask for volunteers to pick out words that they had not heard of before. Explain these words to the class. (A trencher was a piece of bread used as a plate. It was eaten as part of the meal.)

◆ Look at the expression *nightfall* and ask the class what this means. Do they think it is an expressive word; what idea do they think is behind its meaning? Ask the children to compare it to the phrase *night falls* in the next paragraph.

◆ Ask the children to look at each paragraph in turn and try to explain its meaning.

◆ Do the children understand the word *guest*? Do they know what *rushes* and *a harp* are?

◆ Look at the paragraph about washing feet. Have the children heard of this custom before? They may have read about it in the Bible. Discuss how this was not just a custom in Wales, but in other parts of the world too. Why do the children think people had this custom? (For practical reasons, such as keeping homes clean, or as an act of hospitality in order to make guests feel comfortable.)

History activities

◆ Look up with the class where Pembrokeshire is on a large-scale map of the British Isles.

◆ On a simple timeline of British history, mark the lifespan of Gerald of Wales (c.1145–1223).

◆ Remind the children what visitors first did when they went into a Welsh home. (For example, they handed over their weapons to the host.) Discuss with the children how travelling in those days was very different from nowadays. (Most journeys would be on foot or horseback; travelling was not safe, and people took weapons to defend themselves.) Ask the children to guess why it was not very safe in those days. Organise a role-play activity, where visitors arrive and are entertained in a Welsh home in the past. A second role-play could be about visitors arriving in a present-day home.

◆ Look at the illustrations of the traveller, home and girl playing a harp. Show the children other pictures of harps. Explain how the Welsh harp is different from others.

◆ Build up a collection of resources on Welsh history and domestic life, and allow time for the children to browse through the pictures. Set specific questions for the children to research, such as *what foods were eaten at this time; how did people dress; what were ordinary homes like; what were Welsh castles like, what were their names?* Find suitable websites that the children can also use for reference.

◆ Provide art materials for the children to illustrate in their own way the scenes described by Gerald. Make a class display of their collected information and work.

Further literacy ideas

◆ The children to put new or archaic words into their word books or wordbanks and to learn their meanings. Check they have remembered the meanings at the end of the lesson.

◆ Using the information in the text, challenge the children to rewrite several sentences in the first person, as if they themselves were the guests. Model the first few sentences for them, for example *We arrived early in the day, and we were entertained by girls playing harps until nightfall.* Add some of these sentences to the class display, perhaps enlarging the text and changing it into an archaic font.

◆ Create a simple chart containing two columns. In the first, narrower column, list the paragraphs, one to five. Organise the class to work in pairs and to note in the second column what they think is the main point of each paragraph, for example *paragraph one: in Wales people like to welcome others into their homes.*

◆ Ask the children to write a description of their own about a visit they themselves have experienced.

Mary Queen of Scots

Genre
reference text:
a timechart

1542 ~ Becomes Queen of Scotland when only six days old. Sent to live in safety at the French court, after a battle with the English, which the Scots lose. While her mother rules Scotland for her, Mary lives happily in France, with friends of her own age.

1547 ~ Married to King Francis II of France. She is now Queen of Scotland and France, and also has a claim to be Queen of England. Is now a great danger to Queen Elizabeth in England.

1559 ~ Francis II dies. Mary has to leave France to live in Scotland, which she does not remember at all.

1560 ~ Marries Lord Darnley and becomes very unhappy.

1566 ~ Her friend David Riccio is murdered by Darnley, who is jealous of him.

1567 ~ Lord Darnley is found murdered. People in Scotland think Mary and her new friend the Earl of Bothwell planned this murder.

1567 ~ Marries the Earl of Bothwell.

1567 ~ The people of Scotland become angry with Mary and make her son King James VI of Scotland.

1568 ~ Escapes to England and is imprisoned. Many people in England think she is a threat to Queen Elizabeth. They think her supporters will try to kill Elizabeth. Parliament calls her 'the monstrous huge dragon'.

1568–86 Kept in different prisons and castles in England. People beg Elizabeth to have her executed, but she is Elizabeth's cousin, and Elizabeth will not agree.

1586 ~ Writes a letter to Anthony Babington. Mary seems to accept his plan to kill Elizabeth. Elizabeth has to agree to Mary's execution.

1587 ~ Beheaded at Fotheringay Castle. Elizabeth cries for many days.

Mary Queen of Scots

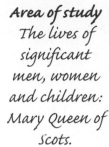

Area of study
The lives of significant men, women and children: Mary Queen of Scots.

History learning objectives

◇ To place events and objects in chronological order (1a).

◇ To use common words and phrases relating to the passing of time (1b).

◇ To identify differences between ways of life at different times (2b).

◇ To find out about this time in the past from text (4a).

◇ To select from their knowledge of history and communicate it in a variety of ways (5).

Background notes

Many English Catholics never accepted Elizabeth as their rightful queen. They supported her Catholic cousin, Mary Queen of Scots, the granddaughter of James IV and Margaret Tudor. Mary became Queen of Scotland as a baby, and after an English victory over the Scots in 1547, she was sent to live at the French court while her mother ruled Scotland for her. She seems to have had a happy childhood with several friends of her own age to play with. By 1559 she was married to Francis II of France, and was Queen of Scotland and France. She also had a claim to the English throne because of her Tudor ancestors.

After the sudden death from an ear infection of Francis II, however, Mary could no longer remain in France and had to return to Scotland – a country she did not know at all. Mistakenly relying on the support of a weak husband (Darnley) and then a series of unpopular lovers (Riccio, Bothwell), Mary failed to establish herself as a stable ruler. Eventually she was forced to escape from serious rebellion and crossed the border into England. Elizabeth was in a difficult position. If she sent Mary back to Scotland it might lead to her death, but if she allowed her to return to France, this might make her a danger. To solve this dilemma, she had Mary imprisoned. Mary remained a prisoner in England for 19 years. For many years Elizabeth resisted pressure from her councillors and Parliament to have Mary executed. Mary was her cousin, but also Elizabeth could not afford to take any action that might be unpopular at home and create international tensions. Eventually, however, in 1587, Mary Queen of Scots was beheaded, increasing the threat of invasion by Catholic countries such as Spain.

This text is set out chronologically, in chart form, and uses an abbreviated note form to convey factual information briefly and simply. As a source for history, its main value is in the chronology and sequence of events, which show clear causal links. Similarly in literacy, sequence is a key feature of the text. There are opportunities for imaginative storytelling and story writing as follow-up activities, based on the brief outline of events it presents.

Vocabulary

Queen; safety; rule; claim; murder; imprisoned; threat; supporters; executed; cousin; beheaded.

Discussing the text

◇ Explain how Mary Queen of Scots is a very famous figure, especially in Scotland. Discuss why this was. (For example, because she had a claim to be Queen of England; her life was full of adventures.)

◆ Read through the chart to the class, then with them. Ask for volunteers to read individual lines.

◇ Ask the children what is special about this kind of text. What do they notice about the way it is organised on the page?

◆ Have they noticed anything about the way it is written or about the style of writing? Discuss the abbreviated style, written in note form. On the board, show two or three sentences based on the information in the chart, but written in full, for example *Mary becomes Queen of Scotland when she is only six days old*. Ask for volunteers to point to words that are included in the full sentences, but missed out of the notes. Can they still understand the notes? What do they have to do when reading the notes? (For example, work out what the missing words are.)Which words are usually missed out? (For example, *Mary* and *she*.)

◆ Discuss what we call the numbers in the left-hand column. What do the children notice about them? (For example, that they are in a sequence; the numbers get bigger, and the date gets later in time.)

◆ In what ways do the children think this kind of information is useful? (For example, it is very clear and it is easy to see what happened and when.) Are there things we cannot find out from it? (For example, we are not given any reasons for any of the events.)

◆ When do the children think Mary was probably most happy? When do they think she began to be sad? When do they think she was most unhappy? Talk about Mary's childhood and how she grew up abroad far from her mother.

◆ Read through the chart of events again.

History activities

◆ Discuss the series of events on the chart and place them on a simple timeline of British history.

◆ Collect stories about Mary's life and adventures and read these to the class.

◆ Discuss why she was popular with some people but also unpopular with some; discuss the fighting at the time between Catholics and Protestants, how Elizabeth was Protestant and Mary Catholic, and how many people in England wanted a Catholic queen. Discuss how, at the same time, many Protestants in Scotland wanted a Protestant ruler rather than a Catholic queen.

◆ Discuss and explain why Mary was sent to France as a small child. (For example, to escape the English Protestant conquerors in Scotland; to be brought up as a Catholic.)

◆ Scan in the chart on the computer and add new information about Mary as it is discovered from wider reading.

◆ Read the Background notes and other information prior to taking the 'hot seat' in the role of Mary. Allow the children to ask you questions about your life.

◆ Use books, resource packs and the Internet to find pictures and portraits of Mary. Print these and use them for art work and for display. Use the portraits to discuss Mary's appearance. Discuss what can be found out from them about the kind of person she was. (For example, they may work out from the portraits that Mary was very attractive, proud and rich.) The children can also write short descriptions of Mary, based on her portraits.

Further literacy ideas

◆ Explain difficult words and ideas to the children during shared reading time, such as *claim to the throne*, *threat to Elizabeth*, *executed*, *beheaded*.

◆ Select some of the points from the chart to copy and give out to the children. Ask them to work in pairs and to write out each point in the form of a complete sentence.

◆ The children write a short story of Mary's life in the first person. Model the first few sentences before they begin, for example *I was born a long time ago, in 1542. When I was only six days old, I became Queen of Scotland.*

George Frideric Handel

Genre
recount text;
modern
fictitious
letter

Friday, July 19th, 1717

My dear John,

What a great success it was on Wednesday!
King George and all his attendants spent the
evening in their barges on the river, listening to my
'Water Music'. The whole river was full of barges. One
entire barge was needed for the musicians. I had 50
instruments of all sorts playing my music all the way.
As you know, John, I had composed these pieces
specially for this occasion.

His Majesty liked the music so well that he asked
for it to be played three times on the river trip, and
then again during his supper at Chelsea. On the way
back, he had the music playing till he landed back
home.

Your very best friend,

George Frideric Handel

Area of study
The lives of significant men, women and children:
George Frideric Handel.

George Frideric Handel

History learning objectives

◆ To place events and objects in chronological order (1a).
◆ To use common words and phrases relating to the passing of time (1b).
◆ To identify differences between ways of life at different times (2b).
◆ To find out about this time in the past from text (4a).
◆ To select from their knowledge of history and communicate it in a variety of ways (5).

Background notes

George Frideric Handel was born at Halle, in Saxony in 1685, and died in London in 1759, aged 74. He was born in the same year as Bach, lived in a similar area and had a similar family background. However, Bach remained in the same part of Germany all his life and brought up a large family on a relatively small income, while Handel never married and became successful and well-travelled, mixed with the aristocracy and wrote music for the King of England. However, Bach is now much more well-known as a composer, and his works are performed more regularly than those of Handel's, many of which have now faded into obscurity.

Handel's *Messiah*, *Water Music* and *Music for the Royal Fireworks*, however, are all still well-known. He wrote *Water Music* in 1717, for King George I of England, to accompany a boat trip on the Thames. His *Music for the Royal Fireworks* was written to accompany a huge fireworks display in London held in 1749, to celebrate a peace treaty with France.

This fictitious letter to a friend aims to give children an insight into the life of Handel at the time of the writing of *Water Music*, and the excitement the commissioning and successful performance of this piece must have generated in the young, ambitious composer. It introduces children to letter form and provides opportunities for them to look at an account written in the first person and at other features, such as the use of capital letters.

Vocabulary

Friend; success; barge; river; entire; musicians; instruments; composed; His Majesty.

Discussing the text

◆ Play some of Handel's *Water Music* to the class. Discuss how this music was written a very long time ago.
◆ Read through the text to and with the class.
◆ Ask the children what kind of text it is. How do we know it is a letter?
◆ Who do the children think wrote the letter? *Who was it to? Why was it written?*
◆ Ask: *What is Handel telling his friend in the letter? Who is the important person that the music was written for? What does 'His Majesty' mean?*
◆ Do the children think Handel enjoyed the experience? How do they know?
◆ Discuss where this is taking place and tell them the name of the river – the Thames.
◆ Why do the children think this piece was called *Water Music*?
◆ How many times do the children think that the king had the music played?
◆ Read through the letter again, and listen to some more of the *Water Music*.

History activities

Ask the class to look for a date in the letter; what date can they see? On a simple timeline of British history, find the place for 1717 and mark on the *Water Music*.

Tell the children about Handel, how he came to live in England from Germany and probably changed his name from George Friedrich Händel or Haendel to George Frideric Handel. His friend John Smith did the same; his name had been Johann Schmidt in Germany.

Look at a map of London and find the Thames, to see where the barges went.

Tell the children how Handel also wrote some *Music for the Royal Fireworks*. If possible, play them some of this piece to compare with the *Water Music*. Discuss the differences between the pieces of music and organise materials for the children to paint and draw water or fireworks pictures.

◆ Using reference books, resource packs and the Internet, find pictures of Handel. Discuss his costume and appearance; look at other people from this period and collect pictures. What is different about the way Handel dressed compared with a man in the present day? Discuss the wearing of wigs. Make a display of the pictures and drawings the children have produced.

Organise extension activities for small groups of children to look up the names of other music composers. Make a list of these to add to the classroom display, perhaps on the timeline.

◆ As a class, investigate types of popular entertainment at this time, for example boat trips.

Further literacy ideas

During the shared reading session, discuss the meaning of all the new or difficult words with the class.

◆ Look carefully at the text and ask the children to point out all the capital letters. Discuss the use of the capitals in each case. Count how many different ways capital letters are used in this text.

Point out to the class the use of inverted commas around 'Water Music'. Ask the children if they can think why these have been used in such a way. Get the children to write brief sentences of their own, quoting the name of a piece of music or a book, and using inverted commas.

Working in pairs, the children compose a brief letter to a friend. Model the layout of the letter for the children before they begin to write.

Nelson's first farewell

Genre
recount text; children's fiction recount from a 19th-century magazine

Once, when he was a small child, Nelson had been playing with his friends but lost his way home and was alone for a long time. Even as a small child, Nelson began to show his great courage. When his grandmother said, "Horatio, you must have been full of hunger and fear." Nelson replied, "Fear? I never saw fear. What is it?"

Later, when he was 12 years old, he said to his uncle, who was a sea captain, "Please let me go to sea in your ship, uncle."

"Let him come," said the captain, who thought Nelson was not strong enough to go to sea, "and the first time we go into battle a cannon ball may knock off his head."

"I am not afraid of that," said the brave young Horatio.

Nelson was still at school when he was called to join his ship. He was sad to leave his brother and grandmother. This was his first farewell, but he said, "I will be a hero and brave every danger!"

Nelson fought bravely, winning many battles at sea. He became first a captain, and then a famous admiral in the navy. Sadly, he was killed during a battle with the French. Even as he lay dying on his ship, his famous last words again showed his bravery, "Thank God, I have done my duty!"

Adapted from 'Nelson's first farewell' in Little Folks *(a children's magazine) 1899.*

Nelson's first farewell

Area of study
The lives of significant men, women and children: Horatio Nelson.

History learning objectives

◆ To place events and objects in chronological order (1a).
◆ To use common words and phrases relating to the passing of time (1b).
◆ To identify differences between ways of life at different times (2b).
◆ To identify different ways in which the past is represented (3).
◆ To find out about this time in the past from text (4a).

Background notes

Horatio Nelson (1758–1805) became an Admiral of the fleet and the national hero of the wars against France during the time of Napoleon. In 1798, Nelson was famous for his victory in the Battle of the Nile, where he destroyed nearly all of Napoleon's fleet off the coast of Egypt. By this stage, he had already lost his right eye and right arm in battle. In 1801, he defeated the Danish fleet at the Battle of Copenhagen. This was the famous event, when Nelson ignored the signal to withdraw – he put his telescope to his blind eye and said, 'I really do not see the signal'. In 1805, the battle to win control of the seas came to an end when Nelson defeated Napoleon's invasion fleet. On 21 October 1805, Nelson caught the French fleet at Cape Trafalgar, off the Spanish coast. He sent a signal to the fleet, 'England expects that every man will do his duty'. Nelson's force, using novel tactics which created havoc among the enemy, destroyed their fleet, killing 4500 men and taking 20 000 prisoners. During this battle, Nelson was shot and killed aboard HMS *Victory*, just at the moment of victory. HMS *Victory* is now docked at Portsmouth.

The story is useful as a history activity because it is about Nelson's childhood, and the children will be able to relate to this. It is written in a chronological sequence and has a clear beginning, middle and end. It also allows children to look at several examples of direct speech and related punctuation. It is also interesting because there are two periods to discuss here – Victorian and Georgian. In Victorian times, Nelson appeared constantly in reports and stories; he was the archetypal hero. Yet, although famous and well known for over a century and a half, he is now little known. This change in our historical interest is an issue for discussion in its own right, and provides an opportunity for comparison with the people present-day children consider famous.

Vocabulary

Courage; sea captain; begged; cannon ball; hero; admiral; duty.

Discussing the text

◆ Ask the children if anyone has heard of a man called Nelson. Have they heard of Nelson's column? Explain how this is in London, in a place called Trafalgar Square. Tell them a little about Nelson if they have never heard of him. Show them the pictures of Nelson and his ships.
◆ Read through the text to and with the class, discussing any difficult words.
◆ Ask the children what had happened to Nelson when he was a small child. Ask them if they can remember being lost. How did they feel? Discuss what Nelson's grandmother meant when she said she thought he must have been *full of hunger and fear*.
◆ Ask: *How do we know Nelson is brave from the first words he says in the story?*

◆ Ask volunteers to suggest and point out any other sentences which show us how brave he is.

◆ Ask if anyone can tell you what a *cannon ball* is.

◆ Ask: *When did Nelson make his 'first farewell'? What does 'farewell' mean?*

◆ Can the children tell you what happens to Nelson in the end? Do the children think he remained brave to the end? How do we know?

◆ What do the children think Nelson meant when he said he had done his duty? Discuss how doing your duty was thought to be a very important thing in Victorian times. What would the children be doing in school if they were *doing their duty?* (For example, working very hard and learning a great deal from their lessons.)

◆ What do the children think the writer is trying to make us think about Nelson? Explain how the writer is trying to persuade the reader in this story. Point out such phrases as: *great courage; I never saw fear; I am not afraid of that; brave young Horatio.*

◆ Read through the story once more.

History activities

◆ Use the Background notes above along with other sources of information to find out more about the life of Nelson, and tell the children the story of his life, including some of the famous events, such as when he put his telescope to his blind eye. Ask them if they have ever heard the expression *turning a blind eye. What do they think it might mean?*

◆ Make a class collection of resources about ships and seafaring in the 18th and 19th centuries, including visual sources and materials from CD-ROMs and the Internet. Encourage the children to browse through the resources and look at the pictures.

◆ Find the date of the Battle of Trafalgar (1805) on a simple timeline of British history and mark it on, perhaps using the symbol of the crossed swords. Alternatively, make a card for this date and a brief caption to hang on a washing-line style timeline across the classroom. Children can add more events and people to this line as they discover information about them.

◆ Divide the class into small groups to find 'clues' about issues such as the following: Napoleon Bonaparte, Horatio Nelson, ships, the lives of sailors now and at the time of Nelson, the Battles of the Nile, Trafalgar and Copenhagen. Give the groups cards to write labels or captions about their findings. When each group has finished, put the findings on the cards into a sequence and get each group to say a little about their cards.

◆ Take the 'hot seat', perhaps wearing an eyepatch, in the role of Nelson, and encourage the children to ask questions about Nelson's life and adventures.

◆ Discuss the notion of the 'hero' or 'heroine'. Ask the class if they can find when the story was written; point out how long after Nelson's death this was. Tell the class how the Victorians loved telling stories about famous heroes. Do they think that this is perhaps why Nelson was so famous at this time? Can they think of any heroes or heroines? Make a list of those they suggest.

Further literacy ideas

◆ Ask the children if they notice anything special about the way the words spoken by Nelson are written. Point out the first set of inverted commas. Explain that these are used to show the reader that someone is speaking. Ask for volunteers to find other sets of inverted commas. *How many are there altogether?*

◆ Challenge the children to think of a person they know of who they think is famous, and to write five or six sentences about them, working individually. They can exchange their writing with a partner to read.

George Stephenson's *Rocket*

Genre
recount text;
recount of
historical
event

The crowds were enormous that week in October 1829 at Rainhill. The gentlemen all wore top hats and the ladies wore brightly coloured gowns and hats. Bands were playing. People were talking loudly, children playing, and all kinds of carriages, carts and gigs were travelling along the roads nearby. There was a large platform so that all the important visitors, like the Duke of Wellington, would be able to get a good view. Flags and ribbons fluttered in the breeze.

There was to be a competition: the organisers wanted to find the best locomotive or steam engine that could then be used to pull trains full of passengers.

George Stephenson was there. He had already made an engine that could travel at 15 miles an hour pulling carriages full of people and trucks full of coal. Mr Stephenson was looking very tense and busy. He was the chief engineer at Rainhill, for he had been asked to put down the tracks on which the engines were to run in the competition.

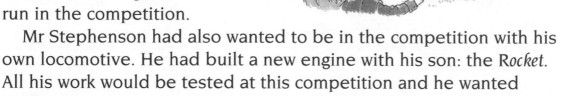

Mr Stephenson had also wanted to be in the competition with his own locomotive. He had built a new engine with his son: the *Rocket*. All his work would be tested at this competition and he wanted to win!

There were two other locomotives in the competition, the *Sans Pareil* and the *Novelty*. The *Sans Pareil* broke down on her eighth trip up and down the short track. The crowds, however, cheered for the *Novelty*, which was small and neat. It went up and down with its red flag flying, but after the second trip there was a loud bang. The boiler had blown up and the *Novelty* was out of the competition. Only the *Rocket* remained. Would she be able to please the judges?

Of course she did. The *Rocket* went up and down the track with no difficulty at all. The crowds were delighted. They cheered and waved their hats, as the *Rocket* did an extra trip along the track to please them. Even the Duke of Wellington stood up to cheer and wave his hat as the *Rocket* passed by. At one moment she reached a speed of 29 miles (58 km) an hour! Did all the spectators know what an important day it had been?

George Stephenson's Rocket

Area of study
The lives of significant men, women and children: George Stephenson.

History learning objectives

◆ To place events and objects in chronological order (1a).

◆ To use common words and phrases relating to the passing of time (1b).

◆ To identify differences between ways of life at different times (2b).

◆ To find out about this time in the past from text (4a).

◆ To select from their knowledge of history and communicate it in a variety of ways (5).

Background notes

The first person to invent the steam locomotive was Richard Trevithick in 1804. The locomotive could move on rails pulling wagons using the power of steam, and it soon replaced the use of horses for both freight and passenger transport. Others developed Trevithick's technology and, during the next half century, railways became the main form of transport, overtaking the canals, which had been of central importance in the previous century.

George Stephenson pioneered and popularised the idea of steam travel with the demonstration of his new locomotive, *Locomotion*. In 1825 he demonstrated to excited crowds how it could pull 12 coal wagons and 21 passenger coaches on the Stockton and Darlington track. Crowds flocked to see the demonstration, which was led by a man on horseback carrying a flag. Soon, as the locomotive gained speed, Stephenson had to call to the man on horseback to leave the lines, because he was being overtaken.

George and Robert Stephenson's *Rocket* won the 1829 Rainhill trials to find the fastest locomotive for the Liverpool–Manchester Railway. This was to be the world's first passenger railway and it began to operate, using the *Rocket*, in 1830. Very rapidly, the idea of carrying passengers on the railway grew, and thousands of miles of track were laid across Britain. Later in the century, the British were also laying track and setting up steam railways in many parts of the world, such as India, Africa and South America.

This story describes the event and the excitement it caused in 1829, just as a similar event had done four years earlier. The extravagance of people's dress, the music and the grandstand for the VIPs helps children to begin to understand a little of the way of life in those days, when any public event would draw large crowds. Developments in transport before and after this time provide opportunity to study the notion of continuity and change. Descriptive terms appear in it, some of which will sound very archaic to young children, such as *gigs*, *gowns* and *top hats*, and there are opportunities to look at the use of capital letters, particularly in the names of the locomotives.

Vocabulary

Enormous; top hats; gowns; carriages; gigs; passengers; tense; chief; tracks; spectators.

Discussing the text

◆ Read through the text with the class, explaining new or unusual vocabulary to them.

◆ What kind of text do the children think this is? Point out the way the text is divided up on the page, into paragraphs, and look at paragraph one. Can a volunteer tell you what paragraph one is about? (It describes a scene.) Can someone tell you what paragraph two is about?

Ask for volunteers to point to the paragraph where the competition begins. Can they tell you where we find out what happened to the *Rocket*?

Discuss with the children how stories often set the scene before the action begins.

How are the children able to recognise the names of the locomotives? What is unusual about one of these names, *Sans Pareil*? (It is in French and means 'without equal'.)

What do the children especially remember about the day the *Rocket* won the competition?

History activities

Ask the children if any of them have travelled on a steam train. Where was this? Can they remember when it was and how old they were? Can they remember what it was like? Discuss what it is like on a steam train – the noise of the engine, the dust and sparks, and the smell of the coal.

Place the dates of Stephenson's demonstrations on a simple timeline of British history, noting how long ago it was. On a large map of Britain, find Liverpool and Manchester.

Talk about the way transport has changed. Ask the class what transport was used before the trains were invented. (For example, horses, carriages and boats.) Ask what they think has changed about trains now; what 'makes them go' nowadays? What other kinds of transport can they think of that we have today? Why do the children think transport continues to change?

Collect pictures and text about steam trains from books, resource packs and the Internet. There is also information available on CD-ROMs.

Ask the children to think of questions they have about this topic, for example: *What happened during Stephenson's first trials of his steam engine? Who invented the steam engine originally? What happened to Stephenson's engine after the competition? What did George and Robert Stephenson do when their engine was chosen to pull the first-ever passenger train? What did George Stephenson look like?* Ask the children to get into pairs or small groups to look up the answers to their questions. Spend some time sharing the answers to the questions at the end. Collect their work in a class book.

Read stories about trains, for example *Thomas the Tank Engine* stories by Rev W Awdry or *The Railway Children* by E Nesbit in whole-class sessions.

Make a frieze about earlier Victorian forms of transport, for example canals or horse-drawn carriages.

Further literacy ideas

Select the 'old-fashioned' words related to this topic for the children to learn their meanings and add to their word books or wordbanks.

Challenge the children to invent appropriate names of their own for new locomotives.

Select children to point out the capital letters in the text. Ask them to explain why a capital letter has been used in the examples they pick. Discuss the different reasons why capitals have been used in this extract.

Give the children cards or slips of paper with dates and events related to the beginnings of the railways. Ask them to make a simple timeline or timechart using their information. They will need to organise their information chronologically. If this is a new idea for the children, provide them with a suggested diagram to begin with.

Look at the elements in the text that give it atmosphere. Ask the children to identify words and phrases that contribute to this.

Look at how the names of the trains are in italics. Ask the children why they think this is.

Grace Darling

Genre
*narrative
text; recount
of historical
event*

It was a dark, wild September morning. The year was 1838. All night a gale had been blowing and the rocky Farne Islands were lashed with spray. Grace Darling was the 22 year old daughter of the keeper of the Longstone lighthouse. She had been helping her father make everything safe during the storm. Her father, who had been up all night, had gone to rest and Grace was on watch alone. There always had to be someone beside the great light, in case it went out.

Grace peered out across the wildly tossing sea. Suddenly she saw a strange shape on the rocks. She knew that this must be a wrecked ship.

It *was* a ship with about sixty passengers on board. In the storm, the ship had been driven onto the sharp rocks. With a terrifying crash, it split in two right across the middle. Most of the passengers were swept away and drowned, but twelve people clung to the wreckage, waiting for daylight to come.

When the tide fell, Grace and her father saw people who had climbed onto the rock. There was no lifeboat in those days and Grace's father knew that boats from the shore could not reach the people in such a storm. His boat needed three strong people to work it and there was only Grace and her mother to help him. Grace wanted to go with her father. She was quite small and this would not be easy for her.

So they set off in the heavy boat. The wind screamed overhead and cold numbed their fingers. They were soaked with the sea and rain. The boat was nearly filled with water as it was lifted high on the towering waves and then sank between them.

At last they got near to the rock. All the people rushed to get in the boat, nearly making it sink. While her father told them that only half could leave on this first trip, Grace had to hold the boat steady, so that it was not smashed against the rocks. She managed this without help.

They took five survivors on board, who helped to row the boat to safety. Her father went back for the others in the boat, and Grace was able to stay behind and help those they had saved. The shipwrecked travellers owed their lives to this brave girl.

THE LIVES OF SIGNIFICANT MEN AND WOMEN

Grace Darling

History learning objectives

◆ To use common words and phrases relating to the passing of time (1b).

◆ To find out about this time in the past from text (4a).

◆ To select from their knowledge of history and communicate it in a variety of ways (5).

Background notes

The story of Grace Darling and her brave determination to rescue the survivors of a shipwreck is a very famous one. It probably gained its fame in this early Victorian period because what she did was considered an extraordinary feat of strength and courage for a young girl in an age when middle-class girls and women were considered too weak and delicate to survive such an experience. The notion of courage and heroism was, of course, supremely important in the 19th century. This story, no doubt, was one of many of the same kind read by a middle-class audience in newspapers and magazines. (See, for example 'Nelson's first farewell', page 112).

The story follows a simple chronological sequence, and provides an opportunity to look at the notion of 'beginning, middle and end'. The use of vocabulary is exciting and evocative, providing a good model for children to use in their own writing. The text allows exploration of the concept of change in people's lives, and also encourages children to use skills in sequencing and the use of language related to the passing of time.

Vocabulary

Gale; keeper; lighthouse; watch; wrecked; passengers; tide; lifeboat; survivors.

Discussing the text

◆ Look at the picture of the storm at sea and the wrecked ship. Discuss what has happened here.

◆ Read the story through to and then with the whole class, discussing the meaning of new or difficult words.

◆ Discuss with the class what kind of text it is. How do we know it is a recount?

◆ Discuss the beginning, middle and end of the story.

◆ Ask the children: *Who was Grace Darling? Where did she live, and what did her father do? How did Grace help her father?*

◆ Can the children tell you how many survivors there were and what happened to them?

◆ Can the children suggest why Grace Darling has been remembered as a special person? Have the children heard of other people who have helped others bravely like this?

◆ Read the story again together, pointing out the language that describes the weather and storm.

History activities

◆ Ask the children if they can see a date in the story; get one of them to write this date on the board. On a simple timeline of British history, find where 1838 is, and discuss how long ago this adventure took place.

◆ Talk about the lives of women and girls like Grace in these days. *Were they the same as today? Did girls do hard and dangerous things nearly two hundred years ago? What sort of things were girls from* comfortable homes expected to do? (For example, work in the home, light tasks, such as needlework.) Compare this with jobs and activities which girls can do today. Discuss how this might have made Grace's adventure more extraordinary to people in those days who heard about it. Get the children to draw up a comparison chart, in which they list: work done by women in the past versus work done by women in the present.

◆ Pick out the key events from the story and cut these sentences out. Paste them onto strips of paper or card for the children to sort into the correct sequence. They can then draw simple pictures to accompany each event, and finally retell the story using their sequence cards and pictures. Encourage them to use words such as *when*, *then*, *at last*.

Provide non-fiction resources for the children to refer to. Set them specific tasks based on the resources, such as *find pictures of ships from the early 19th century* and get them to make their own drawings of them.

Organise small groups for the children to re-enact the drama in their own words. Collect musical instruments to make sound effects representing the wild sea in a storm, and use these to accompany the drama.

◆ Dress in 19th-century style clothes and take the hot-seat in the role of Grace or her father. The children can question you about the events and your feelings on that morning.

◆ Provide paints, pastels and collage materials for the children to recreate the stormy seas and the shipwreck in their own pictures or scenery for their drama.

Further literacy ideas

◆ Which words tell us what the sea was like that morning? For example *wildly tossing*, *towering waves*. Challenge the children to think of other words to describe a stormy sea.

Organise the class to work in pairs to write sentences in their own words about the key events in the story, giving a beginning, a middle and an end.

Provide the children with simple folding booklets containing three or four pages, in which to write a simple series of events about a brave adventure they have heard of. Suggest examples, such as the teacher who saved her class from a gunman; stories about brave people from films or TV programmes they have seen.

Genre
narrative text; autobiography from the past

Mary Seacole

My mother was, like very many of the women who lived in Jamaica, a very good nurse. She looked after the officers of the army and navy when they were stationed at Kingston. I saw so much of my mother, and of her patients, that I really wanted to be like her. So from childhood I wanted to know about nursing.

Then I began to make use of what I had learned from watching my mother. I practised being a nurse upon a great sufferer – my doll.

I made good use of my dumb companion and friend, and whatever disease was in Kingston, you can be sure my poor doll soon caught it. Later, when I was grown up, I had many triumphs as a nurse, and saved some valuable lives. What had really made me most happy though was my first patient's toy face, which I would imagine glowing with health after I had saved it from a long and dangerous illness.

Mary Seacole

History learning objectives

- To place events and objects in chronological order (1a).
- ◆ To use common words and phrases relating to the passing of time (1b).
- To identify differences between ways of life at different times (2b).
- ◆ To find out about this time in the past from text (4a).
- To select from their knowledge of history and communicate it in a variety of ways (5).

Area of study
The lives of significant men, women and children: Mary Seacole.

Background notes

Mary Seacole was born during the time of slavery in Jamaica. She ended her life quite prosperously and was buried in London in 1881. She was perhaps the most highly respected black woman in Britain when she died, as a result of her excellent work with the sick and wounded soldiers in the British army during the Crimean War (1854–56). During the war, Mary Seacole lived on the front line with the troops, risking her own life to care for the army's casualties. She shared with them the horrors of the war. Returning from the war, Mary became renowned for her great work and was befriended by the Princess of Wales, for whom she subsequently worked.

The text gives children an insight into Mary's childhood and the games she played. Children will readily identify with her childhood activities, and will be able to begin to understand the continuity in peoples' experiences as well as the changes that take place over time. The text opens up opportunities for further work on nursing and medicine at the time, as well as into the career of Mary Seacole. Her work could be compared with that of Florence Nightingale, who worked in the Crimea at the same time, and with modern-day nurses, in a study of change between the mid-19th century and the beginning of the 21st. The text has been adapted and simplified from the original, but still provides a challenge for children in appreciating the different style and use of vocabulary in 19th-century writing.

Vocabulary

Nurse; officers; army; navy; stationed; patients; dumb; companion; triumphs.

Discussing the text

- Read through the text to and with the whole class, discussing difficult words or phrases, such as *dumb companion*.
- Ask the children who they think wrote the text. Ask: *What is it about?*
- Can the children find any clue as to when it was written?
- ◆ Can the children work out where Mary Seacole grew up. Can they point out where it says this in the text? Ask the children if we have to 'work this out'. It does not directly say that Mary grew up in Jamaica, but this can be inferred.
- Ask the children: *Why did Mary become interested in looking after sick people?*
  Who was the 'great sufferer'? Why did Mary's doll have to suffer so much?
  What happened to Mary when she was grown up; what phrases in the text tell us this?
  What was the most important memory Mary always had about her nursing?
- ◆ Re-read the text and check that the children now understand the more difficult words and phrases.

◆ Ask the children if they ever play nurses with their dolls.

History activities

◆ Discuss the idea of nursing; have the children ever heard of any famous nurses? Have they ever been looked after by a nurse themselves?

◆ On a map of the world, find Jamaica and see if Kingston is marked on it. Explain how Kingston is the capital city of Jamaica. Next find the Crimea and discuss how far Mary had to travel.

◆ Find 1854–56 on a simple timeline of British history and mark on it the Crimean War; discuss how long ago this was. Look at the date of Mary Seacole's autobiography. How long after the war did she write her story?

◆ Provide an outline, in simple sentences, of Mary's life and tell the story to the class. Once the children have understood the main events, cut up the sentences and ask the children, working in pairs, to put the sentences into the correct sequence. They can stick the sentences onto paper, or into small books and draw illustrations of her life to accompany them. Simple stories about Mary Seacole are available.

◆ Look at the pictures of the wounded soldiers in the Crimea and the conditions in which they were treated. Talk about the problems Mary Seacole must have faced.

◆ As an extension activity for the more advanced readers, provide reference books and opportunities to use CD-ROMs and the Internet, to find further information about the Crimean War, Florence Nightingale, nursing or hospitals during the 19th century. Ask the children to make brief notes on the information they find to add to a class discussion or feedback session.

◆ Discuss the changes in nursing and hospitals that the children have noticed. *What has changed among the things that nurses did 150 years ago and what they do now? What has stayed the same?*

◆ Create a simple chart for the children to complete, showing these similarities and differences.

Further literacy ideas

◆ Talk about how the text is written in the first person; Mary wrote this herself. Ask the children to find as many words as they can that tell us it is in the first person.

◆ Challenge the children to write three or four sentences about Mary Seacole, but in the third person. Model the first one of two before they begin, for example *Mary was born a long time ago. She grew up in Jamaica.* Discuss which words the children will need to change in their sentences, to change them from first to third person.

◆ Ask the children to write about the things they would like to do when they grow up.

Mahatma Gandhi

Genre
information
text; a
newspaper
report

The India Daily News

January 31st, 1948

Ghandi killed
Indian leader shot dead at prayer meeting.

All India is in shock at the shooting yesterday of Mahatma Gandhi, as he was on his way to a prayer meeting. India has lost a great man.

Gandhi was famous for his ideas and for the way he led his own life. When he was a young man he studied law. He believed we should never tell lies, and always tried to be truthful himself. He believed that all people should be treated in the same way, wherever they came from, especially the 'untouchables'. Gandhi tried to live like the poor people of India.

He only had a few possessions, such as his book of sacred hymns, his watch, his glasses and his writing box. Gandhi was very kind and gentle. He loved animals and believed that people should not eat meat. He had been taught this by his Hindu religion and by his parents. He would often fast for a long time.

He always dressed in very simple clothes that could be made by hand. He wanted the people of India to make more things for themselves by spinning and making their own clothes instead of getting them from Britain. For much of his life, Gandhi would spend time sitting spinning himself.

Gandhi wanted India to be a free country, but he did not believe in fighting or using violence. He also wanted people with different religions to live in peace together. Once he nearly fasted to death when Muslims and Hindus were fighting each other. He was able to make them stop, but this was what led to his own death. He was shot by one of his own Hindu people because they thought he was being too kind to the others.

Mahatma Gandhi will live on in people's memories. He will be remembered as one of the world's most famous people.

Mahatma Gandhi

Area of study
The lives of significant men, women and children: Mohandas Karamchand Gandhi.

History learning objectives

◆ To place events and objects in chronological order (1a).

◆ To use common words and phrases relating to the passing of time (1b).

◆ To find out about this time in the past from text (4a).

◆ To select from their knowledge of history and communicate it in a variety of ways (5).

Background notes

Mohandas Karamchand Gandhi (1869–1948), known as 'Mahatma Gandhi', was a Hindu and born into the third highest caste in India. At this time India was a colony of the British Empire. Many Indians lived in poverty, partly because the influx of British goods, particularly textiles, had undermined traditional Indian textile production. Gandhi became acutely aware of this and made it one of his aims in life to re-educate Indians into producing their own clothes as they had done in the past.

After qualifying as a lawyer in London, Gandhi gained employment with an Indian firm in South Africa. He soon discovered that Indians were not welcomed by the white settlers in South Africa. One day he was pushed out of a train when he refused to give up his seat for a white person. This convinced him of the need to fight for the rights of minorities, although all his life he kept to the principle of never using violence in a struggle. Very soon he became leader of the Indian Campaign for Home Rule. Gandhi was sent to prison on several occasions for this work but he never gave up his ideal.

Indian independence was finally achieved in 1947, but to Gandhi's dismay, this led to further conflict between Hindus and Muslims, which erupted into serious violence in many parts of the newly independent country. Gandhi's strategy of threatening to starve himself to death was effective; he quelled the violence in many districts. However, in January 1948, he was assassinated by a Hindu extremist, who thought he had gone too far in appeasing the Muslims.

The piece gives an opportunity to look at the history of a significant person from another part of the world, as well as encouraging children to consider a number of moral issues. There is therefore a close link with both multicultural and citizenship education. This text provides a newspaper 'front page' format for the children to investigate, while at the same time giving a brief overview of some of the main features of Gandhi's life, for which he is fondly remembered. The children can look at the size, style and layout of the text in the article, and at the abbreviated note form of the first few lines.

Vocabulary

Daily; shot; prayer meeting; shock; law; believed; possessions; fast; spinning; violence; Hindu; Muslim.

Discussing the text

◆ Before looking at the text with the class, read the background notes and talk to the children about Gandhi. Look at a map of the world and find India on it. Ask if any of the class have been there, or to Pakistan or Bangladesh.

◆ Read the text to and with the children. Discuss any difficult words with them as they read, such as *fast* and *free*.

◆ Look at the layout of the text. What kind of text do the children think it is; have they seen anything like it before. Provide a current newspaper front page and see how it compares.

Discuss the size of the letters or 'print'; notice how the print becomes smaller and less bold as it goes down the page. Ask the children why they think this is. Why is the headline the biggest? (To catch the reader's attention and allow them to move on to the rest of the article quickly.)

As a class, discuss what is meant by *ideas* and *beliefs*. *Why did Gandhi have these ideas?* (Because of the way his mother had taught him.)

Discuss with the class how Gandhi always dressed as if he were a poor man from India. Ask: *Why did he never try to buy things and become rich?* (He believed we should live simply like the poor.)

Discuss the idea of religious beliefs. Point out how the two major religions in India were Hindu and Islam (Muslim) and how they had become enemies.

◆ Ask: *Why did Gandhi believe we should not eat meat?* (It was part of his religion.)

History activities

On a simple century timeline of British history, mark the dates of Gandhi's life (1869–1948).

Discuss how India was a colony of Britain when Gandhi was young; it had been taken over by the British, many British people lived there and many British things were sold there. India was part of the British Empire. Refer again to the map of the world and ask for volunteers to find India.

Make links with other parts of history which the children might have touched upon, such as Victorian Britain; point out that at the time of Gandhi's birth and when he was young, Queen Victoria was Queen of England and also Empress of India. Introduce language related to the passing of time, such as *long ago*, *in the time of*, *when*.

◆ Provide materials and information so that the children can do some simple hand spinning and weaving.

Look at video clips, CD-ROMs, and other pictures of Gandhi; describe his appearance.

Provide books, pictures and information on different religions, particularly Hinduism and Islam. Discuss some of the key features of each religion

Further literacy ideas

Ask the children to think of words they could use to describe Gandhi, from what they have seen and heard about him, for example *thin*, *small*, *shy*, *kind*, *gentle*; can they add words of their own they think appropriate. Word-process these in different large fonts on the computer, for display purposes.

Give the class some sentences giving news stories, for example *the first man landed on the Moon today*. Ask the children to write the news as in gripping headlines, in note form, for example *first man on Moon*.

Begin with the class a book about important people. Give the children differentiated activities about Gandhi, such as writing captions, sentences or short stories, to work on in pairs and add to the book.

Past events

Image © NASA

The importance of relating history to the current understanding and experience of young children has been taken as a key principle in the selection of the texts in this chapter. They have been drawn from different times in the past, while at the same time relating to yearly anniversaries, or to events which are well known to children for other reasons. They have also been chosen for their links with examples cited in the curriculum or in the QCA scheme of work for History at Key Stage 1.

Most children will hear about Columbus and the discovery of America at some point in their education. The initial incidents in this most momentous time in world history are worth retelling to children, and the original notes made by Columbus himself convey the monotony of the voyage, the anxiety of the sailors and the eventual excitement of that event better than any other text. Transcribed by a Spanish historian in the 16th century, the original text is too detailed and difficult to engage the interest of young children, however. It has been abridged here, but the remaining extracts have been rewritten as closely as possible to the original, in an attempt to retain the feel of the original.

The gunpowder plot and Remembrance Day are regular anniversaries in England. The first verse of 'Gunpowder treason and plot' is well known, and children will be absorbed by the story behind the rhyme. 'In Flanders Fields' is less likely to be known by the children and may prove challenging reading for them, but its close association with the anniversary and with the emblem of the poppy, as well as its own poignant appeal, all make it worthy of inclusion. The Moon landing and the invention of television will need no explanation, and hopefully the words of those closely involved at the time with these remarkable and influential events will inspire their young readers to research further into the history that surrounds them.

Each of the events reflected in these texts can be used to introduce key historical concepts which can be drawn out and explained during discussion. The events themselves span different times and different places; they touch on a variety of human experiences, from the extremes of sorrow at the horrors of war to exhilaration at new inventions or discoveries. Most of the text genres are included and there is opportunity to look at rhyme, report and chronological writing. Work on direct speech, the use of alphabetical order in reference text, and abbreviations can be included in the form of Literacy Hour tasks.

A FAMOUS JOURNEY

Genre
narrative
text; modern
translation of
15th-century
text

Friday, 3 August. We set out at eight o'clock and travelled with a strong breeze sixty miles southward, before sunset. Afterwards we changed course to south-west by south, making for the Canaries.

[The ships sailed to the Canary Islands, where repairs were made to the *Pinta*, and they then continued for several weeks, sailing west toward the place where they thought they would find land.]

Friday, 5 October. We continued on our course and went fifty-seven leagues that night and day, since the wind freshened in the night. I said forty-five to the men. The sea was calm and smooth. "Great thanks be given to God," I said. The breeze was very sweet and warm. Weeds none. Birds, many petrels. Many flying fish flew into the ship.

Saturday, 6 October. We kept on our westward course for forty leagues in the day and night, saying thirty-three leagues to the men.

Sunday, 7 October. We continued on our westward course. Up to an hour after sunrise we went twenty-three leagues, but told the men eighteen. All the ships sailed at the utmost speed in order to be the first to sight land. They all wanted the reward that had been promised to the first person to sight land. At sunrise that day the *Niña*, which was ahead of the others, hoisted a flag at the masthead as a sign that they had sighted land, for this was the order I had given. In the evening, the ships joined each other, but did not see the land that the sailors on the *Niña* thought they had seen. A great flock of birds came from the north and flew south-west. I thought they were going to roost on land. I decided therefore to steer south-west before sunset.

Monday, 8 October. In the day and night together we went about twelve leagues south-west. We found the sea as smooth as the river at Seville. "Thanks be to God," I said, "the breezes are as sweet as in April at Seville, it is a pleasure to breathe them, they are so laden with scent."

The weed seemed very fresh; there were many small land-birds and we took one which was flying south-west. There were terns and ducks and a booby.

Tuesday, 9 October. We made eleven leagues by day and twenty in the night, and told the men seventeen. All night we heard birds passing.

Wednesday, 10 October. We sailed south-west, and went fifty-nine leagues, which I counted as no more than forty-four for the men. Here the men could bear no more. They complained of the length of the voyage. I encouraged them as best I could, telling them about all they would get. I added that it was no use complaining. We had reached the Indies and must sail on till we discovered land.

Thursday, 11 October. We sailed south-west and ran into rough seas. We saw petrels and a green reed near the ship. The men of the *Pinta* saw a cane and a stick, shaped, it seemed by an iron tool. At these signs, all breathed again and rejoiced. We went twenty-two leagues. The *Pinta*, sailing ahead, now sighted land and gave the signals I had commanded. I myself saw a light, and was quite certain that we were near land. I urged the sailors to keep a good lookout for land.

Friday, 12 October. Two hours after midnight land appeared. This was Friday, on which we reached a small island. Immediately some people appeared and I went ashore. I raised the royal standard and the captains carried two banners with the green cross, flown on all our ships. I declared that we had taken possession of the island for the King and Queen and this was written down. Soon many people of the island came up to us.

Adapted from the 'Digest of Columbus' Log Book', by Bartolomé de las Casas

A famous journey

History learning objectives
◆ To place events and objects in chronological order (1a).
◆ To use common words and phrases relating to the passing of time (1b).
◆ To identify different ways in which the past is represented (3).
◆ To understand how to find out about this time in the past from text. (4a).
◆ To select from their knowledge of history and communicate it in a variety of ways (5).

Background notes
Columbus' discovery of the Americas is, of course, not the first to be known about, but it is, perhaps, the most famous. The Vikings are thought to have landed in Newfoundland, Irish monks to have crossed the Atlantic, and the Portuguese to have sailed to Central America before Columbus undertook his famous voyage. Indeed, even during his lifetime, Columbus was denied the acknowledgement of discovery, the honour going to Vespucci Amerigo, after whom the continent was officially named. The only reason Columbus' name is remembered in history is because of the biography written about him by his son, who no doubt felt cheated of the huge rewards promised to Columbus and his heirs by the crown of Spain. These were never received, despite protracted efforts by the Columbus family.

The original log of the journey is lost and this adaptation is based on a 'digest' made by a well-known Spanish historian of the time, Bartolomé de las Casas. Parts of the 'digest' are written in the third person, by de las Casas, but interspersed with sections from the original. To avoid confusion, therefore, this extract has been written entirely in the first person, as Columbus' original log would have been. As such, it provides a chronological account of the last few days before the final sighting of land in the Caribbean islands and will be recognisable to young children as a form of 'diary'. Dates and words to do with the passing of time as a central feature of work based on the text, and there is an opportunity to look at different interpretations of both the event and of Columbus himself. The diary format provides opportunities for related work in literacy, focusing on the use of the first person and a consistent recording system, using days of the week and dates as a reference system.

Vocabulary
Journey; course; leagues; petrels; boobies; frigate-bird; gull; utmost; reward; masthead; roost; laden; terns; bear; discover; cane; signals; urged; lookout; ashore; standard; banner; possession.

Discussing the text
◆ Talk about journeys with the class. What journeys have the children been on? Have they heard of any famous journeys? (For example, Marco Polo; the first man on the Moon.)
◆ Begin by looking carefully at the layout of this text. *How is it organised?* Note how it is set out like a diary, according to the days of the week.
◆ Read the text to and with the class, explaining any difficult or confusing words and phrases.
◆ Ask the children if they can work out who wrote the text; tell them his name was Christopher Columbus and that this is from part of his ship's 'log' or diary of what happened on the voyage.
◆ Look at a map of the world; find where Columbus sailed. *Where are the Canaries?*

◆ Why do the children think that Columbus did not tell the sailors the real distance they had gone? (For example, the men would be afraid and want to turn back, which is what actually happened near the end of the voyage.)

◆ *Why did Columbus think that the way the birds were flying was important? What does 'roosting' mean? Where would the birds roost?*

◆ *Why did Columbus say to his men that they must go on till they found land?* (For example, they would not have enough supplies left to go back to Spain, so they had to go on.)

◆ *What did Columbus do as soon as he found land?* (Claimed the land for Spain.) Do the children think this was the right thing to do? *Why did he do it?*

History activities

◆ Using a simple 'century' timeline, show when Columbus' first voyage took place. (1492)

◆ Refer back to the map of the world and see if volunteers can trace his journey from Spain to the Canary Islands and then to the Caribbean.

◆ Copy and cut up the text or some sentences selected from the text and then organise the children in pairs or small groups to re-order it in the correct sequence.

◆ Gather further resources about the discovery of America from books, published packs of information and pictures, and the Internet. Divide the children into groups to look up specific information about the voyage, the ships, Columbus himself, the King and Queen of Spain, Ferdinand and Isabella, and the maps that were known about and in use at the time. The children can draw pictures and make notes about their findings, either to put on display, in a class book, or report back to the class.

◆ Carry out further reading about Columbus and take the 'hot seat', in the role of Columbus, allowing the children to ask questions.

◆ Show the class carefully chosen clips from feature films or documentaries about Columbus, such as *1492*, for example small sections where nautical instruments are shown being used; the arrival off the Central American coast and the excitement of the crews of the *Pinta*, *Niña* and the *Santa Maria*.

◆ Find a variety of written accounts and biographies of Columbus to compare, some showing him as a hero (most school texts do this), others critical of his weaknesses, such as *Columbus, his enterprise*, by Hans Koning. Ask the children why they think the writers of these accounts have given such different views of Columbus. *Why are their interpretations so varied?*

◆ Make a large wall display, showing the ships on their journey and including collages of Columbus and his crews. Alternatively, make models of the ships and place them on a relief map showing Spain and America.

◆ Look at pictures of the navigational instruments used at the time, such as the compass, the astrolabe and the log and line. Discuss how they were used and the problems encountered in using them on a sailing ship.

Further literacy ideas

◆ Look at the use of capitalisation for the dates. Give the children other dates and ask them to rewrite them correctly with capital letters.

◆ Point out the use of the hyphen in numbers, for example *thirty-three*, *forty-four*. Working in pairs, the children make up some numbers of their own and write them correctly, using hyphens.

◆ Point out how some of the log is in note form, for example *Weeds none. Birds, many petrels*. Give the children some sentences from the text to rewrite in note form. Model one or two of these before the children write their own notes.

◆ Get the children to keep a simple 'log' of each day's events for the duration of this topic.

Gunpowder treason and plot

Genre
persuasive
text; a
traditional
rhyme

Remember, remember, the fifth of November
Gunpowder treason and plot
We see no reason
Why gunpowder treason
Should ever be forgot.

This is the day they did contrive
To blow up King and Parliament alive
Through God's great mercy they were taken
With a slow fuse and a dark lantern
Holler boys, holler boys,
God save the Queen
Penny for the Guys.

Gunpowder treason and plot

Area of study
Past events from the history of Britain and the wider world: the gunpowder plot.

History learning objectives

◆ To use common words and phrases relating to the passing of time (1b).

◆ To identify different ways in which the past is represented (3).

◆ To understand how to find out about this past event from text (4a).

◆ To select from their knowledge of history and communicate it in a variety of ways (5).

Background notes

After the death of Elizabeth I, James VI of Scotland claimed the throne of England. The Catholics hoped that this new king would bring an end to the harsh laws of Elizabeth's Protestant rule, but their hopes soon faded. While James himself was at first ready to be more tolerant of them, his Council and Parliament were not, and the harsh laws remained. A small group of Catholic plotters decided that the only thing to do was to get rid of the King while he was in Parliament, thus removing both the King and Parliament at the same time.

The King was to open Parliament on 5 November 1605, and the night before the conspirators hid 36 barrels of gunpowder in a cellar beneath the Parliament building. Guy Fawkes hid there, waiting to light the fuse at the right moment. Just in time, however, the plot was discovered and Guy Fawkes was arrested. Fawkes was tortured until he told the truth and eventually all the conspirators were arrested and executed for treason.

The first verse of this rhyme is well known and contains several allusions to the story. It is an anniversary well liked by children because of the fireworks displays and opens up opportunities to discuss the events of the plot, introducing them to some important ideas and events in Britain's past. The second verse was sung locally, often in Essex, and introduces the idea of paying for the replicas of the guys, which were ceremonially burnt as a warning to any others contemplating treason. For work in literacy, there are rhyming words and also some archaic words and phrases, as well as terms from the past still in current usage, such as Parliament. The rhyme is an example of how persuasive text can be used very effectively over many hundreds of years. It also introduces ideas and information relevant to later work in citizenship.

Vocabulary

Gunpowder; treason; plot; Parliament; contrive; blow up; mercy; fuse; lantern; holler.

Discussing the text

◆ Ask the children to read and re-read the rhyme, helping them with verse two. Also, give help in pronouncing hard or unusual words.

◆ Have any of the children heard the rhyme before? Do they know both verses or just verse one?

◆ Ask for volunteers to suggest what they think the rhyme is about. *What was the 'plot'?*

◆ Can they work out from the words what actually happened? Look especially at the lines, *This is the day they did contrive /To blow up King and Parliament alive.* What do they think the plotters were trying to do?

◆ What do the children think the rhyme is asking us to do now? Look especially at, *We see no reason /Why gunpowder treason /Should ever be forgot*, and *Holler boys, holler boys,/God save the Queen.* Discuss how the rhyme is trying to persuade us to join in with remembering the treason of the plotters, and to support the king (or queen).

◆ How do we always remember the gunpowder plot?
◆ *Which day do we always remember?* Can the children find the date in the text?

Get the class to say the rhyme again, with as much expression as possible.

History activities

Tell the children the actual date of the gunpowder plot, 5 November 1605, and mark this on a simple century line or timeline of British history. Discuss how it was in the time known now as the 'Stuart' period, because the king's name was James Stuart. Explain how he was already king in Scotland, when he became King James I of England. Look at a map and ask for volunteers to point out where he came from.

Remind the children when we always celebrate the capture of the plotters. Explain in simple terms why the plotters wanted to kill the King, that he was not listening to them and they did not want harsh laws against Catholics any longer.

◆ Ask if anyone knows, or can guess what *gunpowder* is. Explain how, in those days, guns and canons had to be filled with it. The gunpowder was then lit in order to make the weapons fire.

Explain to the class what is meant by *Parliament*. (A place where the rulers of the country can talk and make new laws.) Can the children guess why the plotters did not like Parliament either, and wanted to blow that up too?

Look carefully at the meaning of the word *treason*; can any of the class work out what it might mean? If not, explain that it is treason to try to kill the king or queen.

Read the Background notes and further information about the plotters and Guy Fawkes, and then take the 'hot seat', wearing a large 'Stuart' hat. In the role of Guy Fawkes, answer the questions the children put to you about what happened on the 4th and 5th of November in 1605.

◆ Collect, or make props and costumes to do with the event, such as a lantern, candles, barrels, large hats and cloaks. Working in small groups of five or six, the children can re-enact the events of the 4th and 5th of November. Once captured, place 'Guy Fawkes' and other plotters on trial, and ask them why they carried out the offence.

Collect information and pictures related to the gunpowder plot, and make a class book about it, choosing an 'editor' to plan the layout of the book. Find different pictures of the plotters, some of which portray them as friendly, while others show them as evil.

Further literacy ideas

Ask the children to find all the rhyming words and to put them into pairs or groups, such as *plot* and *forgot*, *reason* and *treason*. Are all the rhyming words at the ends of the lines? Challenge the children to add other words which rhyme to these, and to read them out at the end of the lesson.

Ask for volunteers to find the words they had not seen before, or words they did not understand, perhaps *Parliament*, *treason*, *contrive*, *fuse*, and add these to their word books or wordbanks.

Using pictures of Guy Fawkes and the plotters, the children write sentences describing their appearance. Try to provide a variety of pictures portraying them differently, to allow the children to compare varying interpretations of what the men were like.

Working in pairs the children write brief scripts for their role-plays. Model the beginning of these with the whole class before they begin.

Genre
persuasive text; a poem from the past

'In Flanders Fields'
A poem for Remembrance Day

In Flanders fields the poppies blow
Between the crosses, row on row,
That mark our place; and in the sky
The larks, still bravely singing, fly
Scarce heard amid the guns below.

We are the Dead. Short days ago
We lived, felt dawn, saw sunset glow,
Loved, and were loved, and now we lie
In Flanders fields.

Take up our quarrel with the foe:
To you from failing hands we throw
The torch, be yours to hold it high.
If ye break faith with us who die
We shall not sleep, though poppies grow
In Flanders fields.

By John McCrae, December 1915

In Flanders Fields
A poem for Remembrance Day

History learning objectives

◇ To place events and objects in chronological order (1a).

◇ To use common words and phrases relating to the passing of time (1b).

◆ To identify different ways in which the past is represented (3)

◆ To understand how to find out about this time in the past from text. (4a).

◇ To select from their knowledge of history and communicate it in a variety of ways (5).

Background notes

Soon after the publication of John McCrae's poem, 'In Flanders Fields', it was a great success. It became the most popular poem on the First World War and was translated into many languages. Partly because of the poem's popularity, the poppy was adopted as the symbol of remembrance for those killed in the wars from Britain, France, the United States, Canada, Australia and other Commonwealth countries. The poppy grows abundantly in the fields of Flanders in western Belgium where most of the fighting took place during World War I.

On 11 November, at 11am, in 1918, the last shot of the war was fired and peace declared. However, McCrae was already dead. Having served in the war in South Africa and in the First World War as an army doctor, McCrae died of pneumonia in January, 1918. He was buried north of Boulogne, not far from the fields of Flanders.

The poem is a challenging one for children at Key Stage 1. They will need considerable support in reading and comprehending the last verse in particular, and teachers may wish to omit this verse from their lessons. However, the poem has an important place in the history of this period, and it does have relevance to children's own lives in its relationship to the anniversary of Remembrance Day. They will have seen the symbol of the poppy and the poem might help them understand why the flower is used in this way. The verses are written in the first person and provide opportunities to look at the use of rhyming words, capital letters and the effects of repetition in poetry.

Vocabulary

Poppies; larks; scarce; quarrel; failing; torch; faith.

Discussing the text

◆ Read the poem to the class and then with them, (omitting verse three if this is considered too hard) explaining any difficult words. When the class have read it through, ask them how they felt as they heard and read it. Does it seem to be a happy poem or a sad one?

◇ Why do they think it seems so sad? What has happened in the story that the poem tells?

◇ Why do the children think the tellers of the story are dead? What has been happening to them?

◇ Discuss the First World War briefly and look at a map to find Flanders, in western Belgium.

◇ Look at the pictures of the fields of poppies in Belgium and France today. Explain how many poppies grow where all the fighting took place. Ask if anyone can think why Remembrance Day is sometimes called 'Poppy Day', and why we buy poppies that are specially made.

◆ Look carefully at particular words and phrases, such as *crosses, row on row*. Ask: *What does this mean? What are the crosses that are mentioned?*

◆ *What are the 'guns below'? What does the writer mean when he says 'the poppies blow'?*

◆ *Why does the writer keep repeating the phrase 'In Flanders fields'?* (For example, to impress this image on the reader's mind; to make the poem sound more solemn.)

◆ If you decide to use verse three, ask the children what the poet is asking the reader to do. (For example, continue the fight with the enemy until the battle is won, perhaps. Maybe they did not want to feel that they were dying in vain.)

◆ Read the poem through again.

History activities

◆ Refer back to the map, and show where much of the fighting in the war took place, in Belgium and France.

◆ Locate the time of the war on a simple century line, or timeline of British history. Mark on a span to show the period 1914 to 1918. Discuss why this is called the first war, and tell the children when the Second World War was. Show where this would be on the timeline.

◆ The children can use the illustrations to draw and make poppies of their own. Ask if anyone has a poppy that has been bought on Remembrance Day. Make a class display of poppies to frame a large printout of the poem.

◆ Ask the children why they think we want to remember a war that took place nearly one hundred years ago. *Why do we want to remember that war in particular and the Second World War too, which is also commemorated on Remembrance Day?* (For example, the very great number of soldiers that were killed. More were killed than in any other war; some people think that remembering such a dreadful thing might help to prevent it ever happening again.)

◆ Discuss the date of the ending of the First World War, 11 November 1918. Ask the children which month of the year November is, that is the eleventh. Explain the meaning of the phrase, *the eleventh of the eleventh of the eleventh* – the eleventh hour of the eleventh day of the eleventh month.

◆ If possible, invite a person with experience of the Second World War to visit the class. Arrange for them to talk about Poppy Day and organise the children to ask them questions.

◆ Listen to music that was popular at the time of the First World War.

◆ Add pictures found from resource packs, books and the Internet, as well as drawings and writing to the display.

Further literacy ideas

◆ Ask for volunteers to point out the rhyming words and get the children to make groups of all those that rhyme, adding more of their own.

◆ During shared reading time, discuss how the normal word order has been changed in some of the lines, for example *In Flanders field the poppies blow.* Ask for volunteers to rearrange the words as they might normally be said, such as *The poppies blow in Flanders field.*

◆ Working in pairs, challenge the children to write a sad verse of their own for the class display. Encourage them to use rhyming words and repetition and to make careful use of capital letters in their verses.

The first television pictures

Baird, John Logie: b. 1888, d. 1946. Scottish, inventor of the first television.

In 1925, Baird saw the first actual television picture in his laboratory. His subject was a dummy, which he called 'Stooky Bill'. Bill was placed in front of the camera and his image was sent to the next room.

Genre reference text; an encyclopedia entry

Baird later remembered what had happened. He said, 'The image of the dummy's head formed itself on the screen with what appeared to me an almost unbelievable clarity. I had got it! I could scarcely believe my eyes and felt myself shaking with excitement.'

© The Illustrated London News

Baird demonstrated his television pictures in 1926. He sent them from one room to another. In 1927, he sent pictures along telephone wires from London to Glasgow. In 1928, he sent pictures from England to America.

In 1930, it was possible to watch television at home, although only a very few people did so. The first British television play, 'The Man with the Flower in his Mouth', was broadcast.

The first television pictures

Area of study
Past events from the history of Britain and the wider world: the invention of television.

History learning objectives

◆ To place events and objects in chronological order (1a).
◆ To use common words and phrases relating to the passing of time (1b).
◆ To identify differences between ways of life at different times (2b).
◆ To understand how to find out about this time in the past from text. (4a).
◆ To select from their knowledge of history and communicate it in a variety of ways (5).

Background notes

By the middle of the 1920s, several experiments into the new idea of creating pictures which could be sent down a telephone wire were taking place. John Logie Baird was the first to produce true television pictures, however. Apart from transmitting pictures across the Atlantic, Baird also produced colour television pictures, as well as working on fibre optics and radar. He was instrumental in obtaining broadcasting time on the BBC.

This text contains features essential for children learning how to use reference materials, such as the use of alphabetical order, the reversal of the word order in names for reference purposes, abbreviations, and the note form of the initial information. There is also an opportunity to look at the punctuation of direct speech. As a piece of history, it will engage the attention of young children, who have a good understanding of the importance of television. It provides opportunities to study change from an age when there was no television and brings them into contact with the excitement of the inventor himself, when he saw the first ever television pictures.

Vocabulary

Inventor; laboratory; dummy; image; clarity; broadcast.

Discussing the text

◆ Read the text to the class, then with them, explaining the difficult vocabulary.
◆ Ask the children what they notice about the first line of the text; what is unusual about it? *Why is it different?* (For example, the parts of the name are reversed, there are abbreviations, the text is in note form.) Where would they see this kind of writing?
◆ Discuss what an inventor does. *Which inventor is this text about? What did he invent? What happened to Baird when he first saw the pictures?*
◆ *What did he do next, in the next two years?*
◆ *What was the first thing to be broadcast on British television?*
◆ Do the children think that John Logie Baird's work was important? Why?
◆ What do they think we have gained from having television available to us whenever we want?
◆ Discuss the meaning of the word *television*; *tele-* means *far*, *-vision* means *seeing*.

History activities

◆ Talk with the children about the time before television was invented and what it must have been like. What do the children think that people did in their spare time? Explain how reading stories aloud, playing the piano and singing, and playing games of all sorts were popular pastimes for the people who were fairly wealthy. Others probably had to spend most of their time working and actually had very little leisure time, even the children.

Ask for volunteers to find the date when television pictures were first seen and when the pictures were sent from London to Glasgow, and then across the Atlantic.

Mark these dates on a simple timeline of British history, noticing how long ago this was.

Cut up the sentences from the text which contain dates. Mix them up and get the children to re-order them, to develop their understanding of dates and sequencing.

Look at a map showing Britain and America, noting how far Baird was able to send his television pictures.

Make a class collection of resources about television and John Logie Baird. Allow time for the children to browse through them, looking at pictures and headings. Set specific questions for them to work on using the resources, such as *Where was Baird born? In what country was this? How many homes have television in modern times?* Make a wall display of the children's findings.

Discuss the children's favourite television programmes and make tallies and bar charts to display the information.

Read the section from *Charlie and the Chocolate Factory*, by Roald Dahl, about Mike TV. What is Roald Dahl saying about TV here? (For example, too much of it is not a good thing, especially if we get obsessed by it and become selfish about what we want.)

Discuss how television can now be sent anywhere in the world, and how this is done, (For example, via satellite.) Tell the children about other work that John Logie Baird was involved in, such as fibre optics. If possible, show them a fibre optic lamp and a video clip showing the use of radar. Discuss how vital radar was in the Second World War and how it is also vital to the safety of air travel today.

Further literacy ideas

Pick out words which are likely to be new to the children, such as *laboratory, image, broadcast*. Ask the children to explain their understanding of these words now they have read them in the text. Get the class to add them to their word books or wordbanks to learn. Make a class dictionary of these words, giving definitions and explanations.

Point out the use of inverted commas. Ask for volunteers to count how many times these are used in the text. Discuss why they are used on each occasion, for example to indicate a name, 'Stooky Bill', to show direct speech, 'I had got it!', and to indicate a title, 'The Man with the Flower in his Mouth'. Working together in a shared writing session, ask the children to suggest other examples like these and write them together, using inverted commas.

Look again at the style of the first words in the text. Working in pairs, the children use this style in writing an invented encyclopedia entry about another famous person or event which they have heard of or which they have learned about.

Moon landing

Genre
narrative/
instruction
text;
conversation
between
astronauts
and ground
control

The astronauts talked to ground control as they were landing on the Moon at a place called the 'Sea of Tranquillity'. This is some of what they said:

EAGLE: Coming down nicely… forward lights on… 40 feet… kicking up some dust… 30 feet… faint shadow… drifting to right a little… OK.

GROUND CONTROL: Thirty seconds.

EAGLE: Light. OK engine stop…

GROUND CONTROL: We copy you down Eagle.

EAGLE: Houston, Tranquillity Base here. The Eagle has landed.

GROUND CONTROL: Roger, Tranquillity. We copy you on the ground. You got a bunch of guys about to turn blue. We're breathing again. Thanks a lot.

When the astronauts first left their landing craft, the Eagle, Neil Armstrong was the first to speak from the Moon to all the people listening back on Earth. This is what he said:

NEIL ARMSTRONG: That's one small step for man and one giant leap for mankind.

Image © NASA

From 'The First Lunar Landing', by Rodney Martin

Moon landing

History learning objectives

◆ To place events and objects in chronological order (1a).

  To use common words and phrases relating to the passing of time (1b).

◆ To identify different ways in which the past is represented (3)

  To understand how to find out about this time in the past from text. (4a).

  To select from their knowledge of history and communicate it in a variety of ways (5).

Area of study
Past events from the history of Britain and the wider world: Moon landing.

Background notes

The moment when man first set foot on the surface of the Moon was broadcast to an estimated 600 million people, or one in five of the world's population. The lunar landing was the culmination of the *Apollo* space project, set up during the presidency of John F Kennedy. The *Apollo 11* mission began on 16 July 1969 and three days later the astronauts were in orbit around the Moon. Neil Armstrong stepped out onto the Moon on 21 July.

'Buzz' Aldrin joined him soon after, and the two men set up a television camera to film themselves putting up the American flag on the Moon. While they were there, they also collected samples from the Moon's surface and carried out scientific experiments. They walked on the Moon for eight hours, and received a telephone call from President Nixon. The *Eagle* then returned to the spacecraft and the return to Earth took place in the Pacific Ocean on 24 July.

This extract from the dialogue that took place between the landing craft *Eagle* and ground control in Houston, Texas, gives firsthand experience of the tension and excitement that accompanied the event. The abrupt, broken instructions and comments show the intense concentration of the astronauts as they steered their landing craft onto the surface of the Moon. A firsthand record of this event, well known to all children, this extract will immediately engage their interest and motivate them to enquire further and read about one of the most exciting journeys of all time. Although brief, there are some challenging features in the text, such as the occasional technicalities, and the Americanisms, which children are used to hearing but not reading. The extract provides an opportunity to study text in a form similar to that of a playscript.

Vocabulary

Astronauts; tranquillity; forward lights; kicking up; drifting; copy you; giant leap.

Discussing the text

  Read through the text to the class, then read it with them.

  Ask the children what they think this text is about. *What is happening in it?*

  What kind of text is it? Who is speaking?

◆ Look at a chart of the planets and locate the Earth and its Moon. Notice how close they seem to each other, but point out that this is really a very great distance.

  Discuss the meaning of some of the unusual words or phrases in the text, such as *ground control, forward lights, kicking up… dust, we copy you, a bunch of guys about to turn blue.*

◆ Look at the style of the writing; what do the children notice about the first things said by *Eagle*? *Why is everything written in such as disjointed, broken-up way?* (For example, this is the way they were speaking at the time, while they were trying to land their craft on the Moon.)

◆ Ask if any of the children have heard Neil Armstrong's words before. Point out the importance and meaning of them.

◆ Allocate three speakers to the parts and a narrator. The narrator reads the writing in italics and announces who is speaking. Each speaker takes the part of either ground control, *Eagle* or Neil Armstrong. The speakers and the narrator each read their parts in a 'performance' of the text.

History activities

◆ Tell the children when the 'space race' began, in the 1960s, explaining how Russia and the United States of America both wanted to be the first to send a man to the Moon. The Russians were the first to send a man, Yuri Gagarin, into space in 1961, but the Americans beat them to the Moon when Neil Armstrong and his crew landed there in 1969.

◆ Mark on a simple century line the dates of Yuri Gagarin's first space flight (1961) and Neil Armstrong's Moon landing (1969).

◆ Ask if any of the children have seen the television pictures showing the landing, or any photographs of Neil Armstrong walking on the Moon. If possible, show the class some of these. Video clips are available on CD-ROM.

◆ Collect books, resource packs, pictures and information from the Internet about the space race and the Moon landing. Allow time for the children to browse through it, then give them specific questions to find out about, for example *What was the full date of the Moon landing? Where were the pictures of the Moon landing seen? What other astronauts were with Neil Armstrong? What did the Eagle look like? How did the Eagle get to the Moon?* At the end of the topic work, ask the children to read out their questions and the answers they have found to the class. Alternatively, get them to word-process them and print them out for display.

◆ Use the text as a script for a short play or piece of role-play, creating the landing craft from cardboard, and making space suits from paper, with papier mâché helmets.

◆ If possible, invite to the class a parent or other adult who remembers hearing or seeing the Moon landing at the time. Ask them to talk about the experience to the children.

◆ Make a large 3-D model of a space rocket using card and boxes, based as closely as possible on the original. Add the correct lettering and labelling to it.

Further literacy ideas

◆ Point out the name of the landing craft and its significance. Challenge the children to think of other appropriate names for a spaceship or landing craft.

◆ During shared reading, notice the layout of the text. Discuss how it is organised in this way so that the reader can quickly see who is speaking and what each person is saying. Give the children other examples of speech, written in prose and ask them to set it out like the example in the text.

◆ Working in pairs, the children continue the text in script form until Neil Armstrong returns to the landing craft to return to his spaceship.

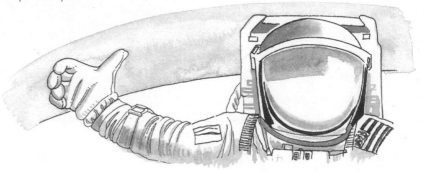